Everyday Life of Medieval Travellers

1 St Christopher and the Christ-child. He is the patron saint of travellers

Everyday Life of
MEDIEVAL
TRAVELLERS

MARJORIE ROWLING

Drawings by John Mansbridge

DORSET PRESS
New York

This edition published by Dorset Press,
a division of Marboro Books Corporation,
by arrangement with B.T. Batsford Ltd.
1989 Dorset Press

ISBN 0-88029-351-9
(formerly ISBN 0-7134-1686-6)

Printed in the United States of America
M 9 8 7 6 5 4 3 2

CONTENTS

THE ILLUSTRATIONS

THE MAPS

ACKNOWLEDGMENT

The author wishes to thank Mr J. J. Bagley of the University of Liverpool, and Dr N. B. Lewis, Emeritus Professor of Medieval History at the University of Sheffield, for generously reading and helpfully criticising the book in typescript.

The author and publishers wish to thank the following for permission to use quotations appearing in this book:

C. G. Coulton, *From St Francis to Dante* and *Five Centuries of Religion*, Cambridge University Press
G. W. Dasent (tr.), *The Story of Burnt Njal*, J. M. Dent & Sons Ltd
R. Hill (ed.), *Gesta Francorum*, Clarendon Press, Oxford
W. Keen, *The Outlaws of Medieval Legend*, Routledge and Kegan Paul Ltd, University of Toronto Press
M. Letts (ed.), *The Travels of Pero Tafur*, Routledge and Kegan Paul Ltd
Iris Origo, *The Merchant of Prato*, Jonathan Cape Ltd
Sir S. Runciman, *The History of the Crusades*, Cambridge University Press
D. Sayers, *The Song of Roland*, Penguin Books Ltd
H. Waddell, *The Wandering Scholars*, Constable and Company Ltd

The author and publishers also wish to thank the following for permission to reproduce the illustrations listed:
The Trustees of the British Museum for figs. 1, 34, 36, 53, 87 and 99
J. E. Bulloz, Paris for fig. 25
The French Government Tourist Office for figs. 3, 4, 6, and 17
Björn Landström for fig. 10
The Mansell Collection for figs. 21, 31, 37, 38 and 40
The National Buildings Record for fig. 33
Lydia Rowling for fig. 41
Thames and Hudson Ltd for figs. 79 and 96 from *The Flowering of the Middle Ages* (ed. Joan Evans)

9

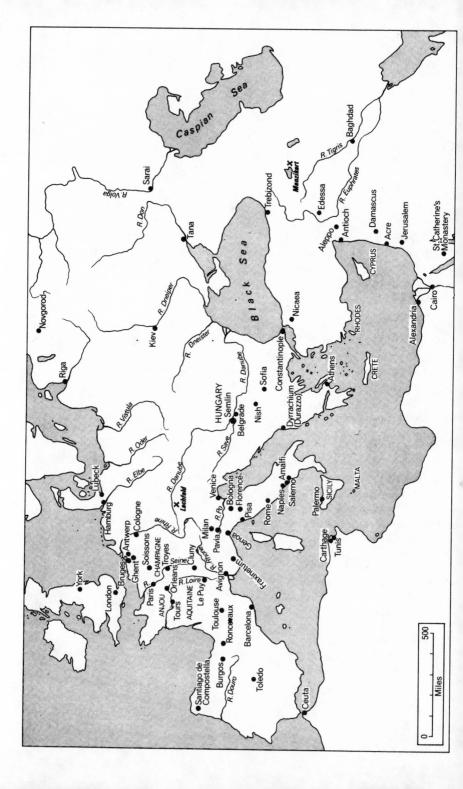

I

Roads, bridges and hospitality

Roads have been for man, not only a means for the traffic and exchange of goods, but highways for the transmission of ideas instrumental in the evolution of barbarism into civilisation. From the state and use made of its roads, the condition of a community can be judged, since their paucity or decay points to a certain inertia and poverty within that community.

Such a period of decadence was developing even before the fall of the Roman Empire, when its splendid system of roads was neglected, when townsfolk fled to the country to escape from crippling taxation and to put themselves under the protection of the nearest powerful landowner. Barbarian incursions completed the decline of most urban centres, and when the Germans became masters of former imperial domains, the peasants accepted their rule and protection, giving in exchange payment in rent or kind or some form of labour or services. Thus western Europe was scattered with manorial estates on which the workers lived in small hamlets near their lord's manor house or fort. Only towns that were the seat of a bishopric, or centred round a Benedictine abbey, or a few that managed to keep up an ancient industry, possessed a modicum of organized urban life. Long-distance trade, except along a few routes, practically disappeared. Roads became increasingly derelict and deserted, being used mainly by war-bands. Barbarian attacks from without and internecine warfare between lay lords and even bishops within, forced towns and villages to strengthen ancient walls or erect earthworks; castles, manor houses, abbeys and many churches were fortified or made capable of affording a refuge to the surrounding countryside.

The military successes of the Moslems made such fortifications even more imperative, for after conquering Syria, Egypt and

3 Fortified abbey of Mont St Michel, France

North Africa in the seventh century, they were only prevented from overrunning the rest of western Christendom by Charles Martel's victory at Poitiers in 732. Their command of the Mediterranean, however, completed Europe's severance from the Byzantine Empire and the east. Attacks from the Vikings in the north-west still further helped to obliterate organized urban life and to turn western Christendom into a self-sufficing series of estates with peasants living in villages under the protection of their lord. Even a once flourishing port like Genoa, sank in this period into a mere fishing village.

Then, during the eleventh century, the west slowly began to emerge from its torpor. Moslem power was not only checked, but was losing ground. The Norse were turning to wide-spread trade with the west, the east and Constantinople. In 955 the Asiatic Magyars of Hungary were defeated by the Germans, so that by the twelfth century a wonderful flowering of European civilisation followed. Had it been possible during that century for a tenth century traveller to journey through this new and expanding Europe, he would have failed to recognize once familiar towns and landscapes. Whole stretches of country, especially beyond the Elbe, had been conquered from backward and pagan peoples, or reclaimed from forest and waste. The heavy plough with coulter and ploughshare, sometimes fitted with wheels, had revolutionised agriculture in the north-west. A new padded and rigid collar enabled the horse to replace the ox as a draught animal and the three-field system was proving much more productive than the Roman two-field rotation. All these changes vastly altered the rural landscape. In addition, new towns had been built with new roads to connect them; stone bridges spanned fords or rivers where wooden structures or pontoon bridges, as at Arles, had been; highways were busy with traffic and trade, while convoys of merchants, pilgrims, students and entertainers, with ecclesiastics, kings and princes and their attendants, journeyed from place to place.

Yet, though attacks from without had abated, internal strife remained both endemic and epidemic in western Christendom throughout the Middle Ages. Large tracts of country, especially in the east, remained unpopulated, and although there was a sudden bulge in population in the twelfth century, Europe never possessed even a quarter the number of inhabitants which swarm in ever increasing numbers over its surface today. One historian has calculated that in 1437 the population of the entire Duchy of Brabant was about 450,000. In 1947 it was two and a half millions. But one should not conclude that the total population of Europe at the end of the Middle Ages was therefore five times less than that of today. In fact it was probably a good deal less, and no figure exists to give an accurate assessment of numbers living at that period.

An increase in population there certainly was, however, which made an increase in food production a necessity, as was the construction of new roads along which food and trade could travel. The wonderful network of Roman roads had for long been neglected and robbed of paving, but main highways had always to be kept in at least a usable condition. In the thirteenth century when the Cistercian Abbey of Vale Royal was built in Cheshire, peasants drove carts, laden with stone, twice daily from a quarry eight miles distant, and made thousands of journeys even during winter. True, stone for building was usually sought in

4 Carcassonne, a fortified town in France

quarries as near as possible to the working site. Failing suitable stone being available near at hand, a quarry was chosen from which stone could be carried by water. Barnack quarries supplied material to the abbeys of Peterborough, Ramsey, Crowland, Bury St Edmunds and Sawtry which was transported mainly by boat. Nevertheless there was a regular transport of materials by cart along the roads of Europe throughout the Middle Ages, and after 1338 a road for the use of small carts was even constructed through the Septimer Pass in the Alps.

How far, then, did kings and governments participate in the upkeep of roads? In Naples, under the Hohenstaufen and Angevin rulers the administrative authority took effective measures for repairing highways. In France, the royal government did nothing for their upkeep. In England, legal and administrative measures were definitely adopted regarding roads, and neglect or obstruction were indictable offences. The Statute of Winchester laid down, for instance, that highways from one market town to another should be enlarged, and bushes, woods and dykes, where a man might lurk to do hurt, be 200 feet away on each side of the road. For in England the law declared each landowner to be responsible for roads which crossed his land. It was, however, also regarded as an act of charity and of merit to aid in the upkeep of roads and bridges wherever situated. Merchants and wealthy men left bequests in their wills for this purpose. Thomas Paycocke, the fifteenth-century English wool merchant, left £20 in his will for 'amending the foul ways between Coxhall and Blackwater'. In 1332, the merchants of Ghent paid for the repair of the highway from Senlis during their lifetime to hasten the passage of their goods to Paris. Tolls, which were heaviest on goods, had been instituted on roads for their upkeep. These were often usurped by magnates for their own use. The exactions then became a greater hindrance to trade than the disrepair of roads.

Goods were carried along the roads in the two-wheeled ox or horse *bronette*. This was more suitable for medieval roads than the four-wheeled *carette*. By the fourteenth century the lighter *cabriolet* was being used for short journeys. Certain districts developed their own form of transport. In England, carriers ran from Southampton to Winchester and to Oxford, while others went from the Cotswolds to London. Agents or 'brokers of carts' existed in London and large towns to arrange for the transport of goods and letters. In the mid-fourteenth century regular

5 Medieval common cart

carriers of wool plied between Flanders and Basle, these being mainly Alsatians and Sarrois. Waggoners from Béarn followed overland routes from Toulouse to the Atlantic seaports, while around Péronne in northern France, colliers yoked to barrows transported goods locally. By the end of the thirteenth century trains of packhorses operated regularly from Italian towns, through the Alps to the fairs of Champagne.

It was largely through these and other fairs that traffic in Europe increased considerably during the eleventh and twelfth centuries, those of Champagne being the most famous. During January roads converging on Lagny were crowded with Flemish, English, Italian and Provençal merchants taking goods to the fair and later returning heavily laden with merchandise they had bought there. In May, the fair of St Quiac in Provins, in June, the 'Warm Fair' at Troyes made the roads equally busy. Then by September a second fair was in full swing at Provins with the 'Cold Fair' of Troyes in October.

The Flemish fairs of Bruges, Ypres, Lille, Thourout and Messines drew merchants across Alpine routes from Italy, carrying spices, silks and goldsmiths' work to buy Flemish cloth which would be transported from Genoa to Levantine ports. For by 1310 the Champagne fairs were declining. The direct shipping of goods from Italian ports to Flanders and England, the conduct of business by correspondence instead of by personal exchange and the industrialisation of Italy, as well as the change from silver to gold in international large-scale trade which disorganised exchange at the fairs, all contributed to their decay.

Important as were roads to the development of trade, bridges also were a vital factor and these during the twelfth century were kept in repair by a variety of patrons. Rochester Bridge in England, built in wood, was rebuilt in stone under Richard II.

The upkeep of the fifth and ninth piers became the responsibility of the Archbishop of Canterbury, that of the fourth was the King's, while the first was shared between the Bishop of Rochester and some neighbouring manors.

In France a special religious order, the *Frères Pontifes*, founded in the twelfth century, built and repaired bridges. The Pont St-Esprit and the famous Bridge of Avignon are among those erected by the Brothers. Royal bridge builders include the English queen Matilda who erected Bow Bridge and granted land to the abbess of Barking so that the rents from the same could be directed towards the upkeep of the bridge and its approaches.

London Bridge, whose fame is still perpetuated in children's singing games, was begun by a priest and chaplain, Peter Cole-church, in 1176. Perhaps tiring of the constant repairs needed to the wooden structure, he began a new one in stone. Soon the king himself and many London citizens were sending donations. In 1201 Peter, now aging, was replaced as director of works by Isembert the famed French master mason. King John, impressed by his splendid bridges at la Rochelles and Saintes, brought him to London. Finished in 1209, the defensive towers of London Bridge, its chapel and the houses and shops built on it became the pride and boast of Englishmen for centuries. Rents from the houses and tolls from passengers, animals, vehicles and goods using the bridge went towards its upkeep. Foreign merchants sailing between the movable drawbridge and the City bank of the Thames, also paid toll. Apparently fines exacted from breakers of the peace swelled the revenues, for in 1301 Nicholas, baker of Cornhill having assaulted a serjeant of London's Mayor was warned that, if he repeated this exploit, he must pay 20s. towards the fabric of London Bridge.

On one of the towers nearest to the drawbridge decapitated heads of traitors were placed. But when this tower was rebuilt in the sixteenth century and named Nonesuch House, it was re-garded as too splendid to be defaced by these gruesome relics, which were relegated to the tower on the Southwark side.

Wealthy merchants sometimes built and endowed bridges. That of the fifteenth-century Sir Hugh Clopton at Stratford-on-Avon, England, still exists. Merchants probably paid for the erection of the Alpine Devil's bridge which was flung across the gorges at Schöllenen in the early thirteenth century, thus opening up the St Gothard Pass route between Italy and northern Europe.

Guilds also repaired roads and bridges. That of the Holy Cross in Birmingham, founded by Richard II, and guilds in Rochester, Bristol, Ludlow and other towns 'maintained and kept in good reparaciouns various stone bridges and divers foul and dangerous highways' in their several vicinities.

Chapels were often built on bridges and dedicated to a saint who reputedly gave special protection to the structure, while chantry priests attached to the shrine prayed for the safety of travellers and those who contributed alms. The chapel on the famous St Bénézet bridge at Avignon is Romanesque in style. In England parts of medieval bridge chapels are still found at Wakefield, Rotherham and Bradford-on-Avon.

6 *The Valentré bridge, Cahors, France*

Bridges were usually fortified, one of the finest surviving examples being the Valentré bridge at Cahors, France, with its three tall towers. The Frères Pontifes incorporated into their bridge at Pont St-Esprit a travellers' hospice which, while retaining its beautiful Gothic portal, was remodelled in the seventeenth century into a Citadel.

Hospices were not the only buildings which gave shelter to medieval travellers. Kings and magnates usually lodged in their own castles and manor houses or else in abbeys or in the homes of their subjects and tenants, for which they were supposed to pay. Monastic establishments, especially those of the Knights Hospitallers were enjoined to provide hospitality for their patrons which led to a considerable impoverishment of their coffers. In 1352 Munchen Gladbach, one of the richest abbeys of north Germany was almost ruined because

neighbouring counts and knights haunt the abbey with their wives and children, their kin and friends. They drink at the abbot's table and his income thereby is so diminished that he is almost compelled to break up his household and leave the place.

7 Abbey kitchen, Fontevrault, France

The great Romanesque kitchen of the abbey of Fontevrault in the Loire valley, surrounded by châteaux, bears witness, with its 20 chimneys and five wood-burning cooking hearths, to the nearness of the great who claimed hospitality, not only for themselves, but for their wives, children, attendants, their horses, falcons and hounds. The poor had a primary claim on monastic hospitality, but many of these preferred a bed of straw in the outhouse of an inn in company with other 'tinkers, sweaters, swinkers, all good ale drinkers'.

Indeed by the twelfth century there were inns and taverns in plenty, many both commodious and sumptuously furnished. Gautier, hero of a French fabliau declares, 'How fine are inns today—what a welcome, what service and compliments. The only drawback is the cost!' Gautier's original 60 sous, his father's gift, soon found their way into the pockets of a group of experienced gamblers in their inn. After losing his cloak, surcoat and horse to them, he was soundly beaten by the innkeeper for his inability to pay his bill, then flung out of doors practically naked. Prostitutes as well as thieves and coiners frequented inns, while jongleurs, pardoners, triacleurs or quack doctors visited them in search of gullible patrons.

An entertaining inn scene is drawn by an Englishman who

wrote a manual to aid his countrymen to speak 'sweet French according to the usage of France'.

Janyn, the servant of a wealthy traveller has ridden ahead to engage rooms for his master. After rousing the inn-keeper, Janyn asks,

> 'Is this inn comfortable?'
> 'As God hears me, it is fit for a King's lodging.'
> The host leads Janyn into a room hung with gold and silver drapes.
> 'I hope no lice, fleas, or vermin have been left here', says Janyn.
> 'The room has been cleaned. You will be comfortable in it,' avers the innkeeper, but adds reluctantly, 'True, there is a great pack of rats and mice about the place. But I've set snares for them, so there should be no trouble.'
> Janyn looks dubious, but orders a fire to be lit. Meanwhile he buys fowls for supper in the market then returns to cook them. When his master arrives a convivial evening begins. Wenches are brought in from the village. More wine, in jewel encrusted basins, as well as copious supplies of beer and cider are provided. Cornet and clarinet players appear. The company dances until midnight.

8 Preparing for guests at an inn

Finally, after bestowing a green silk girdle on his hostess, purses on his host and servants, the traveller and his attendants retire. Janyn, no doubt devoutly hoping that the vermin traps have been effective.

It was through such inns, over these bridges and along the roads of western Christendom that a constant stream of men and women passed from the eleventh to the fifteenth century. To watch this living panorama on the road or travelling by river and sea, is to view the life of these times from an unusual angle. Kings pass marching to war with all the pomp and pageantry of medieval campaigning, bishops ride on visitation with a splendid entourage. Magnates and gentry move from manor to manor 'to live on their own'. Hastening across Europe go merchants and kings' messengers, master masons, carpenters, painters and sculptors ever eager to start on a new cathedral. Furtive and hunted, the serf flees along the road from conditions insufferable on his own manor; here an outlaw spurs to escape justice, there a fugitive prisoner has just reached a sanctuary door. Vagabonds turned pedlar are tramping on the road to wealth, to become merchants both rich and respected. Others, less fortunate, like the English Robert Goodgroom, thief and occasional mole-catcher, become 'running rivers of treason'. Like him they are overwhelmed by waters deeper than they had bargained for, ending on the gallows. But all are travellers who, between birth and death, weave not only their own patterns but add to the warp and woof of European history. For history is indivisible and the medieval tapestry is part of the whole, not a panel irrevocably separated from the rest.

2

Sea-routes, ports and ships

AD 1000 was a date much dreaded in Christian Europe as the year of doom. Yet by then the savage attacks of Moslem, Norse and Magyar upon her were beginning to lessen, though only the Magyars—by the German victory at Lechfeld (955)—had been finally stayed. Byzantine sea-power had also revived and Fraxinetum, the Moslem pirate stronghold in Provence, had been destroyed (975). The Moslems had lost ground also in Spain and on the Mediterranean, while the sea-power and trade of Venice, Naples and Amalfi had increased.

In the north also the Vikings were turning to trade rather than to raiding, and had been granted the dukedom of Normandy by the French king (911), so that by the beginning of the eleventh century Europe was like a sick man emerging after a serious illness into convalescence—a recovery that was marked by increasing movement of shipping and an upward trend in the volume of trade. In the Atlantic, voyaging to Iceland and northern Spain, the open-decked boats of the fierce and valorous Vikings were to be seen, while the Varangians (Danes and Swedes) carried cargoes of furs and amber, wax and jars of honey, with bands of unhappy Slavs roped together like merchandise, all destined for the marts of Constantinople. Their routes to the Byzantine capital from the Baltic followed the great Russian rivers to the Caspian and the Black Sea. On their return journeys the Varangians carried spices, wine, silks of Baghdad, and works of art in gold and silver to sell to the courts and abbeys in the north and west still wealthy enough to buy them. For until the rise of the new German ports in the Baltic, the Swedish *knorrs*, with their straight-ended cutwater fore and aft, and homespun sails, kept from sagging in wet weather, by cross bands of leather stitched on to them, were the main carriers of the north. But

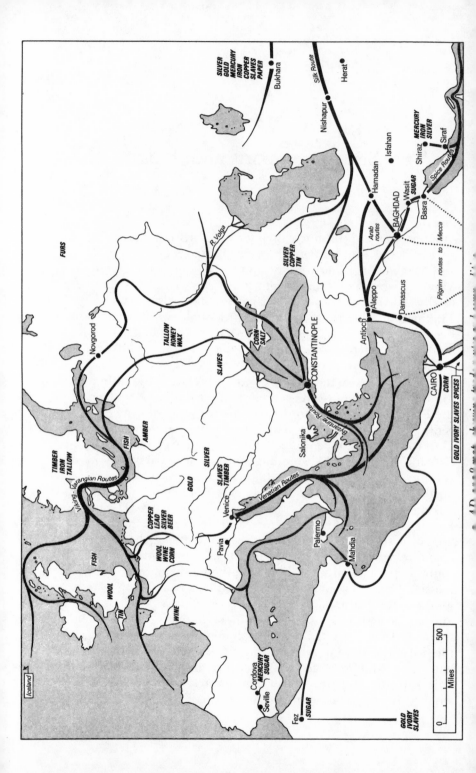

Europe and the Near East c. AD 1000: map showing trade routes and commodities.

Gotland, established by them as a great entrepôt, was to be wrenched from them by the Germans who were pushing steadily eastwards. By 1143, Lübeck — soon to become Mistress of the Baltic—had been established as a purely German town, while Riga, Rostock, Danzig and Wismar followed, with Hamburg in the west at the foot of the Jutland peninsula. So that, instead of Swedish *knorrs*, it was the typical straight-ended vessels, roomy and with a deep draught, known as *coggen* that were then seen in all the chief harbours of northern and western Europe. The Baltic German towns, later joining together into the Hanseatic League, soon developed a corn export

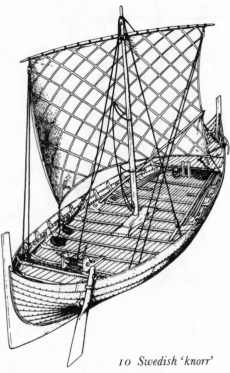

10 Swedish 'knorr'

trade and carried textiles on their return journey to Russia and the Baltic states. So important was the trade of these Hanse towns that in 1180 Bruges built the new port of Damme and by 1293 that of Sluys, expressly to accommodate the *coggen* with their deeper draught.

By 1360 the Hanseatic League was formally established, marking a new phase in the history of European trade and of German power. By the fifteenth century, however, Philip the Good of Burgundy (1419–67) was encouraging the Flemish mercantile marine to compete with the Hanse and was pushing on the development of Antwerp. This city, within a century was to oust Bruges from its position as leading port of the north-west.

But in 1213 the recently made port of Damme was so large that the entire French fleet could anchor there. The town was filled with merchants trading in silver and metal of all kinds. There were also silks from Phoenicia and China, dyes from Hungary, wine from Gascony, wool from England and cloth

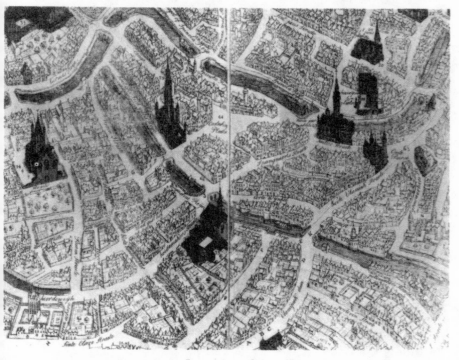

11 Bruges in 1562, trading quarter

from all Flanders. Bruges itself had been fortified after the French occupation of 1301. There were eight gates in the enclosing walls which were further strengthened by ditches, ramparts and towers flanked by canals, so that it was one of the most powerfully protected cities of the period. Watermills and many windmills were erected on rising ground near the new fortifications. The principal streets were paved so that with its palaces and consular houses, its many churches and fine *Waterhalle*, as well as numerous shops and offices of the Hanse, in addition to Spanish, English, Gascon and Bordeaux merchants' quarters, Bruges was as splendid in appearance as she was flourishing in commerce. By 1344, the town was enlarged by additional special streets and buildings to accommodate the personnel of Danish, Hamburg, Norwegian, Portuguese, Spanish and Venetian traders.

Meanwhile, after the Saracen domination of the Mediterranean had been broken in the eleventh century, Venice had been developing her trade to the full. Founded in 811 by refugees fleeing from the Franks, the city was gradually built up on its 117 islands around its splendid basilica dedicated to St Mark and erected during the years 1063–73. But continuously from the ninth to the thirteenth century the merchant princes of Venice added to the splendour of the city in proportion as they increased through conquest and trade its enormous wealth.

Even in the fifteenth century when the shadow of decline was falling over it, Pero Tafur, a Portuguese traveller and pilgrim, wrote from the house of a merchant friend in Venice: 'Every hour news is carried in by ships from all countries in the world. The seaborne traffic is very great.'

Two years later, in 1438, Tafur was again in Venice, but this time on Ascension Day.

The Venetians assembled in the Piazza of St Mark, he writes, arrayed in their best. Then the Doge emerged from his palace in great magnificence. After hearing mass, he and all the clergy embarked on a ship called *Bucentoro*, and sailed out to sea. Here a priest threw out Holy Water, then the Doge, drawing a ring off his finger cast it into the waves.

This ancient ceremony, Tafur explained, was symbolic of the sea's marriage to the land, for since Venice was joined to the sea, it was necessary also to placate the ocean's fury in this way by recognising the union.

Venice enjoyed a gay social life and in this the Doge joined freely as is shown in a fifteenth-century painting where he is depicted sitting with other members of the Senate watching a lively display of bull-baiting in the piazza below. Normally, no four-footed animals were allowed in the streets which Tafur tells us

12 Venice—the Doge watches bull-baiting from the palace balcony

were clean for walking on as a fair chamber, being well paved. The ways are kept free from mud and dust, while the sea washes all filth from hidden places, or the stench would be unbearable. The Venetians, moreover, burn perfume, and spices are crushed in the streets, to emit a fragrant odour.

Venice was threatened for a time by her rival Genoa until in 1380 the latter was defeated in a sea battle by the Adriatic city's fleet. From then, until the advance of the Turks in the fifteenth century she remained leader of the seaborn commerce of the Mediterranean although Genoa retained her control of the Black Sea, gained after the Byzantine restoration of 1261. Tafur visited Genoa also, and gives her high praise.

> We passed along the seashore 40 miles from Genoa which is the most beautiful sight in the world. The whole coast from Savona to Genoa looks like one continuous city. We entered the harbour by the Mole and were cheerfully received by both men and women. The city is very ancient. They say it was founded by Janus, prince of Troy. It is placed upon a very high mountain above the sea. All the houses are like towers, of four or five storeys or more. The streets are very narrow and difficult of access. The soil is unproductive, but the people are industrious. Provisions are imported from all parts of the world. There is an excellent harbour, with a mole, a tower and a lighthouse, which burns all night. On the opposite side is another lighted tower so that entry to the harbour may be known to everyone. . . . The great church is called San Lorenzo. They keep in it the Holy Grail which is made of a single emerald.

Tafur's 'Holy Grail', the *Sacro Catina*, is still preserved in Genoa. It is a cup from which Christ is reputed to have drunk at the Last Supper. Made of dark green Venetian glass, octagonal in shape, it was taken by the Genoese as part of the spoils of Caesarea in 1101 during the Crusades. Indeed, it was largely through the Crusades that Venice, Genoa and for a time, Pisa developed as great shipping centres and entrepôts for trade. In addition spoil and conquests gained through the Holy Wars brought them a vast store of additional wealth. To accommodate pilgrims and crusaders, their stores, weapons and horses, larger and costlier ships had to be built.

These vessels, used in the Mediterranean from the twelfth to the fourteenth centuries, were mainly of three types. Armed galleys, using both oars and sails; the round ship, carrying few, if any arms and using mainly sails, and the *tarida*, heavier and slower than the galley, with a full set of sails, two masts and well equipped with oars. The development of medieval ships can be traced from the seals of various ports, on mosaics, marble reliefs and works of art. Two fundamental differences existed for some time between ships built in the north of Europe and those of the Mediterranean. Whereas the latter were carvel built, with planks placed

13 Seal from Poole, England c. 1325

edge to edge, the former were clinker built, having the edges of upper planks projecting over the lower.

The lateen sail, probably taken over from the Arabs, was triangular and was used in the Mediterranean during the greater part of the Middle Ages. In the north, the square sail was customary. But, by the time that Venice was sending an annual trading fleet to Southampton in the fifteenth century, the square sail was in general use in the Mediterranean, also.

Northern vessels can be studied on the seals of the Cinque Ports and those of other English coastal towns. In the thirteenth century these 'round ships', so called from the shape of their bows, had developed high castles fore and aft. The topcastle and the central sail were square, and an oar type of rudder was still used as in Viking days. A seal from Poole about 1325 shows that the aftercastle had now developed until it had become almost a quarterdeck. Sometimes—as shown on a ceiling painting in the Church at Skamstrup, Denmark—it even occupied all the space aft of the mast and became a partial top deck.

Ships were changing even more quickly in the Mediterranean. During the fourteenth century, instead of the two banks of oars in galleys, pairs of oars were used, in which the rowers sat side by side. The development of trade, and the fact that wealthy merchants often accompanied their goods, led to a demand for bigger and more luxurious travelling quarters. Hence the development of fore and aft castles as cabins. During the Crusades when kings and nobles had to undertake long voyages, the castles became more elaborate and were sometimes fitted with oriel windows as in the fourteenth-century merchantman shown on the tomb of St Peter the Martyr in Milan.

In 1268 Louis IX ordered a number of Genoese and Venetian

ships. One of these may be portrayed on a mosaic in St Mark's. This vessel has three masts—not usual at this date—and two heavy lateral rudders which were so efficient that Joinville, the king's historian, declared that the vessels answered to the helm as easily as a horse to its guiding reins. Extra cabin accommodation was also provided by doubling the decks and having a two-tiered sterncastle. Indeed, thirteenth century ships were surprisingly large. One from Venice, used by St Louis, was 110 feet, overall, maximum beam 41 feet. The largest Genoese—*the Paradiso*—was just over 83 feet.

By the fourteenth century, Genoa and Venice, besides improving their ships, had formulated regulations regarding the equipment, loading, manning and sailing of their armed galleys. These had to sail in convoy under an admiral, who in Venice was appointed by the Senate. The oarsmen were freemen who were allowed to do some trading on their own account. The galleys also carried a fair number of bowmen of whom a certain proportion had to be of noble rank. They were known as 'bowmen of the quarterdeck' and were chosen according to the Senate's decree by competition at the butts in Venice. They were fed gratis at the captain's table with his officers and any wealthy merchants who were on board. They also had the right to take a little cargo without paying freight charges. Thus, to impoverished

*14 Ship of 1268 from a mosaic in St Mark's, Venice,
perhaps a copy of St Louis' ship*

young men of good birth, opportunity was given to gain experience in trade and sea-faring.

The day-to-day life on board the galleys was fraught with danger. Not to life alone, but, to a captain or admiral especially, a wrong decision could mean ruin. Such a catastrophe destroyed Nicolo Barbarigo of Venice. In December 1414, he was commanding a fleet of galleys returning from Alexandria after exchanging a cargo of silver and gold for one even more precious—that of spices. The channels between the rocky Dalmation islands were so treacherous that it was officially forbidden to navigate them at night. But the Christmas fair in Venice was approaching. Doubtless urged on by his officers and crew who all would have a small stake at least in the cargo, Nicolo sailed through the Canale di Zara in the dark. Emerging, his ships were met by the full force of the dreaded northern gale. One vessel was driven ashore, but Nicolo on the flagship, ignoring distress signals, sailed for the nearest harbour. From there he sent a boat to aid the distressed galley. He himself proceeded to Venice. He was tried, condemned for disobedience and inhumanity, and fined the ruinous sum of 10,000 ducats. He died shortly after, leaving his 20-year-old son Andrea to start his career as one of the noble but impoverished 'bowmen of the quarterdeck' on a voyage to Alexandria.

Political storms were also frequent and could be as disastrous as any cyclonic disturbance to the captains of convoys and their crews. Day-to-day decisions had to be constantly made. During the many wars, ships had to put into island harbours to gain news of movements of the enemy, in order to know which route to take. In 1430 one of these political situations arose to test the Venetian traders. The Moslem Soldan of Egypt had monopolised the sale of spices and put up his prices exorbitantly. The Senate took the precaution of buying a large amount of spices, then ordered the admirals of the spice fleet not to unload their goods on their next visit to Alexandria unless the Soldan's terms improved. On arrival they debated the Soldan's assurances, decided they were untrustworthy, raised their anchors and sailed away without a single stroke of business being done. Such loss of revenue brought the Soldan to his senses and the Venetians had no cause for complaint on their next visit.

But already the shadow of more serious threats was approaching the Mediterranean ports. The caravels of Henry the Navigator of Portugal were searching for the sea route to India down the

African coast. Before the fifteenth century ended da Gama had reached India and the Genoese Colombus had begun his third voyage to the Americas. Indeed the Portuguese caravel and the more cumbersome carrack had their sails set, not only for entry into new worlds, but into a new age as well. The Modern Era had begun.

3

Merchants and explorers

Merchants who developed long-distance trade, together with explorers who discovered and colonised new lands, played a major part in the development of the new Europe which began to evolve after the year 1000. Indeed it can be claimed that gradually they helped to undermine feudalism and to free the serf in western Christendom, to create not only a new aristocracy founded on wealth, but a prosperous bourgoisie who built and endowed churches and hospitals, lazarettos, guild halls, splendid town houses, bridges and roads. These new classes encouraged art and also literature written in the vernacular, while through closer contacts with the Byzantine and Moslem world which followed, science and classical learning were restored to the west.

Since, during the seventh to the tenth centuries, the Mediterranean was largely under Moslem domination, it is in northern areas that we must first look for commercial and colonising activities. Early ventures were mainly conducted by the Scandinavian nations. These have been so deeply branded as pirates and destroyers that their work as explorers and traders has been unjustifiably minimized. Yet, in the ninth century Norsemen had

15 Norse ships from the Bayeux tapestry

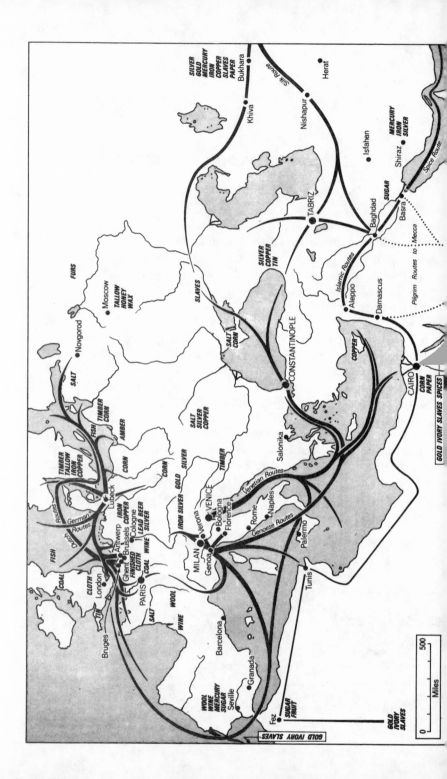

discovered and settled Iceland. From there, in the year 1000, Leif, son of Eric the Red, sailed out one spring morning and eventually discovered a land of green pastures where wild wheat and vines grew abundantly. He called it Vinland. Three years later a second expedition set sail and reached what must have been the coast of Labrador, thus making the Norsemen the discoverers of America five hundred years before Columbus set out towards the west in search of India.

The exploits of these early Scandinavians are most picturesquely portrayed in the Icelandic sagas. Their independence and enterprise, their endurance of unbelievable hardship, hunger, icy cold, toil and danger, their love of battle and the daily life on their farmsteads between voyages, are vividly depicted there. In the *Story of Burnt Njal* we see Njal's sons, Grim and Helgi, setting out with Olaf and Bard the Black on a trading expedition from Iceland.

> They got so strong a wind from the north that they were driven south into the main. Then so thick a mist descended that they could not tell where they were driving. Finally they reached a great ground sea and thought they were near land. Njal's son asked Bard to which land they were likely to be nearest.
>
> 'With the weather we have had, we might hit the Orkneys, or Scotland or Ireland,' he said.

Two nights later they cast anchor. Next morning they saw 13 Viking ships approaching with obvious intent to attack them. After asking the chapmens' names the Vikings shouted, 'You have two choices—one to go ashore while we take your goods. The other that we slay every man we catch.' Helgi cried that they would fight. 'Nay,' some of the chapmen called, 'Lading is less than life.' To drown this 'sluggard's choice', Grim yelled loudly, 'Take your weapons and guard your goods.'

In the middle of the unequal fight, the chapmen saw ten other ships approaching, whereupon they rowed quickly towards them to ask for help.

> Along the sides of the ships were shield on shield. Upon the leading ship stood a man clad in a silken kirtle with hair both thick and fair. He had a gilded helm and held a spear inlaid with gold. He was Kari, Solmund's son.

With Kari's aid the chapmen were able to defeat their Viking foes.

33

More important for western Europe, however, than the northern activities of the Norsemen were those which they pursued to the east and south. By the tenth century they had established Novgorod as a trading centre in Russia. From there, the more adventurous pushed further east and south to the Caspian and Black Seas and to Constantinople. They used the rivers Dnieper, Don and Volga, but this involved dragging their ships over watersheds and refloating them on the further side. By the early eleventh century they had broken the Khazar grip on the trade with the east. In their shallow boats with their blue, red and green striped sails of homespun wool, they carried amber, fur, slaves, wax and honey to the Byzantine and Islamic empires. A vivid picture of the barbaric background to the life of these northerners settled in Russia, as well as proof of the civilising contacts they made with Moslems, has been preserved in a little known chronicle of the Arabian Ahmad bin Fudhlan, who had been sent in 921 by the Caliph Muqtadir, as an envoy to the 'King of the Slavs' in the town of Bulghar on the Volga. These 'Rus', as the Scandinavians were called, traded with Byzantine merchants who brought silk, gold and silver to pay for the northern wares received. Ahmad, who had been sent to teach Islamic law to the Norsemen, was keenly interested to learn about the customs of these northern people. Hearing that a Rus chieftain had died in the neighbourhood, he went to watch the funeral ceremonies, about which he wrote an account on returning to Baghdad.

On the chief's death his wealth was divided into three parts, of which one third went to the family, one third to pay for new garments for the deceased and one third to provide drink for the funeral feast. His servants were then asked, 'Which of you will die with your master?' On this occasion a maidservant volunteered, and spent the following days, while garments were being sewn, drinking, singing, happy and cheerful. Then the Arab traveller continues,

> On the arrival of the day on which the chief and the girl were to be burned, I came to the river. On the bank the chief's boat had been drawn up and was supported on four posts, with wooden figures round it, like tall human beings. Then men placed a bier on the deck and covered it with quilts and satin cushions, supervised by an old woman, dusky, hale and hearty, whom they called 'the angel of death'. Over the bier, the men erected a tent and into this the de-

34

ceased was carried and placed on a couch. He was dressed in new trousers, gaiters, shoes, a tunic, a satin mantle with gold buttons and a cap of sable and satin.

Fruit, food and all his weapons were put at his side, as well as several newly sacrificed animals. The maidservant then appeared and was lifted, so that she could look over a wooden door frame which had been set up on shore. Three times she was raised to peer over it, each time greeting her parents and friends in the other world. After various ceremonies, which Ahmed describes, the girl was lifted into the boat and led by the old crone into the tent. At once a group of men appeared with shields and beat them loudly to drown any screams the girl might make while she was barbarously put to death in the tent. A funeral pyre was built over the boat, and master and maid were burned together.

At this moment, Ahmed wrote, an awe-inspiring gale arose so that the flames grew stronger and fiercer. . . . A man beside me laughed heartily. 'Out of love for him, his Lord has sent the wind to take him away this very hour.' And in truth, an hour had not passed before the boat, the wood, the dead man and the girl were all burnt to ashes. . . . They erected a mound over the place where the boat had stood on the bank and set up over it a piece of wood on which were written the man's name, and that of the king of the Rus.

One of the great Viking travellers of the eleventh century was Harold Sigurdson, son of Olaf, who journeyed to Miklagard (the Great Enclosure), as the Vikings called Constantinople, and became captain of the Varangian guard, in the service of the eastern emperor. The Viking wanderlust took him to Greece, Sicily and north Africa. When he returned to become king of Norway in 1050, he explored the White Sea with a view to expanding trade with Russia in furs. His restless ambition finally drove him with an army to Britain where he was defeated in 1066 at Stamford Bridge.

The Vikings who settled in Ireland were great traders also and the cargoes of their ships is revealed from a list of booty taken after a battle, by the native Irish from the Norse city of Limerick.

Their jewels and best property, saddles, beautiful and foreign, their gold and silver, with beautifully woven cloth of all colours, their satins and silken cloths both scarlet and green.

During the twelfth century as a result of the expansion of Europe's population and boundaries, the establishment of new towns and development of agriculture, trade also increased, and with it the number of merchants. Some of these, who attained great wealth, started from very humble beginnings. Godric of Norfolk is an example. The son of peasants, he was endowed with great physical strength, outstanding intelligence and un- doubted initiative. He decided to forsake the land and became a pedlar, when 'he was wont to wander with small wares round the villages and farmsteads near his home. Then he associated with city merchants and went along the highway through towns and boroughs, fortresses and cities and to fairs.'

As he lived near Spalding on the sea-shore, he collected what was valuable from wreckage and sea-drift, and went to St Andrews, probably on a coastal boat to sell his wares. After a journey to Rome, part pilgrimage, part trading expedition, Godric 'formed a close friendship with other young men who were keen to trade'. This was probably a *compagni* partnership such as was often found in Italy, and about which the fourteenth century merchant Datini wrote,

> What solace, happiness and satisfaction there is between good *compagni* bound to each other by faithful friendship. . . . I believe that two partners or brothers in the same occupation, who act sincerely, will earn greater profits than if they traded separately.

Godric was typical of the merchants of this earlier period in having many different sorts of goods for sale, and in selling them in person. He did not specialise, as the large scale mer- chants in the fourteenth and fifteenth centuries. Nor did he conduct his business as they did through agents established in the great city trading centres. Godric also lived in a period when faith was more ardent and sincere and relied unhesitatingly on the protection of the saints in the many perils he encountered.

> Having learned by frequent experience his misery during these dangers, he gave certain saints more ardent worship, venerating and visiting their shrines. . . . some of his prayers he learned from his fellow travellers . . . others from the custom of the place, for he visited these holy places with frequent assiduity.

He made great profits and joined other merchants in the pur- chase of half of one ship and the fourth part of another. As he

17 Fortified tower of Caesar at Provins

excelled in navigation he was promoted to the position of steersman and received a greater percentage of the profits. Some of these he devoted to the making of pilgrimages to Jerusalem, to Rome, Compostella and St Gilles. Godric ended his life as a hermit at Finchale near Durham, having donated all his wealth to the poor.

During Godric's century the Count of Champagne was devoting himself to the development of trade in his area. Realising the profits he could make by encouraging merchants to attend fairs in his towns of Troyes, Provins and Langres, he helped to organise them as entrepôts where merchants from the weaving towns of Flanders could meet those from the trading towns of Italy, France and Germany. By the twelfth century the Champagne fairs had become so famous that Chrétien de Troyes could write

> *At Bar, at Provins and at Troyes,*
> *You're bound to make a fortune.*

Nevertheless, the lot of the merchant travelling the roads to the Champagne fairs was far from being either safe or easy. Italians had to take their pack-horse trains through the dangerous passes of the Alps, whose hazards are described by the traveller Pero Tafur after crossing by the St Gothard pass in 1438.

> The next day I arrived at the foot of the St Gothard pass, high in the Alps. . . . It was the end of August when the snow melts in the great heat, making the crossing very perilous. An ox, accustomed to the way, goes in front drawing a long rope. To this a trailer is attached, on which the passenger sits, holding his horse behind him by the reins. In this way, if any accident happens, only the ox is imperilled.

There was a danger from avalanches, from swollen streams and rivers, and perhaps more terrifying in the superstitious Middle Ages, the Alps were regarded as the home of restless spirits and terrifying dragons. As late as the seventeenth century travellers gave eye-witness accounts of these reputed monsters one being 'two feet long, with a red, hairy cat's head, sparkling eyes, scaly legs, a tongue like a snake's, and a long, hairy bifid tail'.

Difficulties also arose from the differing currencies of the various cantons, and the possibility of attack by brigands. By the

18 Country traders enter a town

thirteenth century, however, the area and scope of protection provided by the officials of the Champagne fairs was so wide that, in 1242, a convoy of merchants attacked and robbed in northern Italy by bandits from Piacenza, obtained compensation for their losses through the Champagne authorities. They informed the authorities of Piacenza that their merchants would be excluded from the fairs until restitution was made. Needless to say the necessary payments were made without delay.

Not only did Italian merchants travel north with

alum and dyes so necessary for the Flemish cloth trade, but they took loads of precious spices shipped to Italy from the east—pepper and cinnamon, ginger, mace and cassia. There were eastern rugs and silks—23 different types—and sugar of all kinds. In return, they would bring back the world famous cloth woven in Ypres, Douai, Ghent and Bruges—the *Four Leden* of Flanders—and export it from Genoa to Syria and the east, or send it to Florence to be finished by the *Calimala*.

By the end of the thirteenth century the Germans had established themselves in Bruges as the chief exporters of Flemish cloth, and this contributed with other factors towards the ruin of the trade of the Champagne fairs. It was now the turn of the new German towns to take a foremost place in northern commerce. They banded themselves together finally into the Hanseatic League to protect their interests at home and abroad. Nevertheless their methods of trading were always behind those of Italy. One historian declared that in 1500 their development was 200 years behind that of the business houses south of the Alps. The Hanse merchants continued to cling to their home towns, and therefore, to prosecute their business, had constantly to undertake long journeys. Whereas the Italian businessman of later times directed his business through letters to agents and factors in the commercial towns of Europe, the Hanse merchants still accompanied his goods on sea and land. He therefore was referred to as 'Bergenfahrer' or 'Englandfahrer' according to the place for which he was bound.

In the south, even before the opening up of the Mediterranean and the pushing back of the Moslems, Pavia and Venice had been entrepôts for trade. In the early eleventh century English merchants were braving the dangers of the Alpine passes to bring hounds, furs and silver to the markets and fairs of Lombard Pavia. They found customs posts on the Italian side of the passes, and when ten per cent of their goods by way of toll were demanded from them, objected strenuously in typically English fashion. King Canute, however, when attending the coronation of Conrad II in 1027 discussed the matter of trade with the emperor, and it was decided that English merchants 'should not be hindered by so many customs barriers nor harassed by unjust tolls'. In Lombardy however it was agreed that English merchants should pay every three years as toll 'fifty pounds of pure silver, two fine greyhounds with gilded embossed collars, two shields, two swords, two lances, with, to the customs officer in charge, two fur coats and two pounds of silver.'

By the twelfth and thirteenth centuries, Venice and Genoa were becoming great trading powers. A typical trading expedition left Genoa on 8 September 1253 on the *Stella*. There were 14 merchants on board, 15 armed mariners, six of them crossbowmen, with a mate as navigator whom the merchants had chosen themselves. Fifteen days before the ship left Genoa, having been leased for a certain period, the mate was sworn 'to enquire diligently into the equipment. . . . If he shall find anything wanting he is held by oath to manifest to the merchants those things that are lacking.' The mate would check that there were four to seven sails, one of them new and made of canvas, the rest of cotton; that there was an adequate number of extra spars, of ship's boats, anchors, coils of cable and so on. At this period it was not compulsory to sail in convoy. But the *Stella*, after setting sail, decided to call at Malaga for news of conditions in Ceuta, before sailing there. Here they did some trade with the spices and cotton they carried, and the scribe, whom all merchant ships carried, recorded sales, checked the weighing and marking of goods, and worked out the amount of profit due to each merchant. When it was decided that it was safe to proceed to Ceuta they set sail, and spent the winter in pleasure and trade in the port, buying goods to replace those sold. In the spring they voted on whether to go on to Bougia and Tunis before returning home. Sometimes merchants went as far as Syria on this kind of voyage.

By 1318 Genoese and Venetian ships were sending merchant fleets to Flanders. This direct trading with the north dealt another blow at the prosperity of the Champagne fairs. The description of a trading venture sent out by Andrea Barbarigo in 1430 brings out the dangers of these commercial voyages. Andrea was the son of that Nicolo Barbarigo who had been ruined and disgraced by breaking the regulations of the Senate against sailing in the Adriatic at night (p. 29). In 1418, when only 19 years old, Andrea had a mere 200 ducats—his mother's gift—as his trading capital. By 1430 he had retrieved the family fortunes, but decided then to send some merchandise on a cog named the *Balba*, which with four others was sailing to Bruges, with cargoes of Cretan wine. It was cheaper to ship goods by cog than by the galley-convoys organised by the senate. Four cogs arrived safely, but the *Balba* was captured by pirates, and since Andrea had not insured his goods, he suffered a total loss. He had also sent six bales of pepper on one of five galleys sailing for Flanders. These ran into a Castilian war fleet which challenged them. As the galleys were shipping Sicilian goods and Sicily was at war with Castile, the Venetians hastened to send a gift of jewels to placate the Castilian admiral, who consequently allowed them to proceed without searching their vessels. Andrea's pepper and other merchandise arrived safely this time in Bruges, and with the

19 A fifteenth-century sea battle

profits, he bought, through his London agent, 23 barrels of pewter and 23 pieces of English cloth. Their homeward voyage was threatened, however, by the war between Venice and the Duke of Milan who ruled over Genoa, whose powerful fleet was centred on Sicily. By keeping well out from the island they escaped notice and reached Venice safely.

An explosion of journeys of discovery which took place during the thirteenth century opened up the Far East to direct trade with western merchants. These were made possible after an eruption of wild Mongolian hordes had subjected China, taking Pekin in 1214, then surging west conquered Asia, Russia and Poland and penetrated deeply into Hungary. The destruction wrought by these swift and savage eastern horsemen struck dismay into Europe. Then in the 1250s they subjugated the Moslem lands: they destroyed Baghdad in 1258 and extinguished the Caliphate. This changed the attitude of Europeans. If the Tartars could be converted to Christianity they might ally with the west, and sweep the Moslems out of existence. From the mid-thirteenth century, embassies were sent to Persia and faraway Cathay by the Pope, and by the kings of France and England,

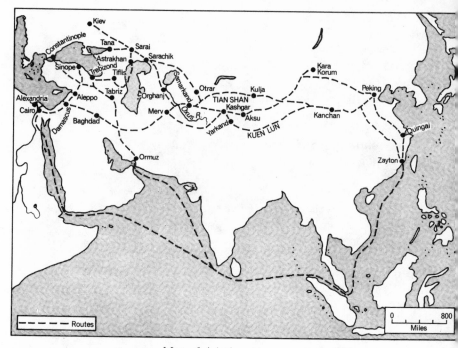

20 Map of Asiatic routes c. 1245–1368

with invitations to the Tartars to become Christians and allies. Merchants followed to trade and friars to convert. The earliest European to reach Karakorum, capital of the Mongol empire, was John of Pian di Carpini, a Franciscan friar sent by the Pope in 1245 on a mission of friendship, with a view to converting the Tartars. John was well over 60 when he set out on this dangerous journey of incredible hardships and privations. On the journey to Kiev he narrates:

> We were feeble even to death, yet continued in a wagon through the snow and extreme cold. . . . In Kiev they told us that our horses would all die in Tartary since they were unable to dig for grass under the snow, like the Tartar horses.

John therefore exchanged their horses at Kiev for post-horses and set out for the Tartar dominions with a guide over the frozen steppes. On reaching the court of Prince Batu they found that, though his dwelling was a great tent, gold and silver vessels were used for all meals which were accompanied by singing and music.

As they were commanded to travel with all speed to the imperial court they 'rose early and travelled until night without eating anything, coming so late to our lodging that often we had no time to eat that same night, but did not do so until next morning'.

On finally arriving at the court of Kuyuk they saw a white tent so huge that more than two thousand men might stand within it. It had painted wooden walls, and the friars watched the Tartar chiefs and innumerable ambassadors assemble to elect the new emperor. A description of Kuyuk's election is given. Fabulous gifts were presented to him—camels and horses richly caparisoned, a sun canopy from Cathay set with jewels, five hundred carts filled with gold and silver, silk girdles, rich robes and costly weapons.

The return journey of Friar John's party was as arduous as the outward one had been.

> We travelled all winter long, lying in the deserts often on the snow ... for there were no trees and the plains were open. In the morning we frequently found ourselves covered with snow driven over us by the wind.

It is not surprising that, as a result of these sufferings, Friar John fell ill after his return and died. But the results of his journey lasted for a century, since Italian merchants were able to trade directly with the east.

From 1253 to 1255 a French Friar, William of Rubruck, travelled on an embassy sent by St Louis of France to contact Sartach son of Bartu, commander of Tartar troops in Russia who had become a Christian. William by the advice of merchants from Constantinople travelled in

> covered carts such as the Russians carry their skins in ... because if I should use horses I must unload and repack my things at every stopping place. Besides I should ride a more gentle pace with oxen drawing the carts. Through their evil counsel I took two months to reach Sartach, which I could have done in one by horse.

William also took pleasant fruits, muscadel wine and delicate biscuit-bread as gifts to the governors of Soldaia. When they arrived at the court of Batu, William writes,

> I was astonished, for his tents stretched like a mighty city for a space

21 Marco Polo leaves Venice

of three or four leagues. In the Khan's pavilion, Batu sat upon a seat like a bed, gilt all over. One of his ladies sat by him. . . . At the entrance to the tent was a bench, holding stately great cups of silver and gold set with jewels.

When they set out for the court of Mangu Khan, the guide said that, during the four month's journey, they would have to endure such cold that stones and trees were split by the frost. Accordingly, the friars were given a furred gown of rams' skin, breeches of the same, shoes of felt and skin hoods. William was always provided

44

with a strong horse 'because I was corpulent and heavy'. 'Of hunger and thirst, cold and weariness there was no end,' he states. The friar writes fully of the wonders of his journey, of 'certain people who eat their own parents', of the splendours of Karakorum, of feasts and ceremonies and divinations, but ends,

> I will tell you confidentially that, if peasants—I do not speak of knights or kings—wanted to travel like the kings of the Tartars, and content themselves with the food of these potentates, they would become leaders of the world.

It was not peasants, however, who endured the privations of the arduous journey to Cathay, but merchants who, if not 'leaders of the world', secured great wealth. Marco Polo is the only trader to leave an account of his travels, but what a colourful and adventurous narrative it is! Pergolotti, however, agent of the Florentine commercial house of Bardi wrote about 1340 a guide for merchants trading in the east. This gives many details of the life and habits of these traders with Cathay. He tells them when they should use horses, when camels or pack-asses on the route.

22 Marco Polo's camel caravan

Provisions and costs are set out, and advice as to dragomen: 'At Tana, hire a dragoman, but do not economise by taking a bad one at less cost. You will save by having a good one.' He also states that the road you travel from Tana to Cathay 'is perfectly safe . . . even when the road is at its worst, if you are some sixty men in your company you will go as safely as if you were in your own house'.

Yet even while Pegolotti wrote, the wheel of Fortune for eastern overland traders was beginning to revolve in a downward direction. The Mongol Empire was falling into anarchy, and the Chinese Ming dynasty, antagonistic to the west, was displacing the Mongols from power. Then in 1343 a Genoese caravan en route for Cathay encountered opposition from the Ottoman Turks. By 1352 these Moslems, bitterly antagonistic to Christians, had captured Syria, Asia Minor and most of the Balkan peninsula. Western merchants were again cut off from their caravan roads to the east. Yet in 1436 the Spanish Pero Tafur met Nicolas Conti in Sinai on the Venetian's return from India. He described the way there as 'very long and troublesome and perilous' so that Tafur decided satirically that if he did not fly there it was impossible to make the journey.

By this date the impetus to find a sea-route to India was gaining momentum. From as early as 1291 when the Vivaldo brothers had set out from Ceuta to find a way by sea to the Far East the idea had never really died. But it was Portuguese sailors, instigated by the enthusiasm of their Prince, Henry the Navigator, who pushed enthusiastically further and further down the African coast until in 1498 Vasco da Gama reached India round south Africa by sea. So that although the land area of Christendom shrank terrifyingly in the fifteenth century, although in 1453 the Turks captured Constantinople after thrusting spear heads through the Balkans into Hungary, although it seemed indeed that advance in the west was grinding to a halt, yet by the intrepidity of seamen explorers, vast spheres of influence and trade were opening up for the west. Indeed Columbus' discovery of America added another continent to the direct influence of Europe. So that it is from the year 1500 that historians, since the eighteenth century onwards, have traced the rise of Europe's domination of the world.

4

Royalty, magnates and messengers

If the king decides to spend the day anywhere, especially if the herald has proclaimed it, he will start off so early in the morning as to throw everything into confusion. Men running about like mad, goading pack-horses, chariots colliding, with a noise like the infernal regions.

Sometimes the king declares he will leave early, then slumbers till noon, while pack-horses droop under their loads, chariots stand ready, couriers fall asleep and everyone grumbles.

But when the king changes his mind about his destination—what chaos! Probably only one horse can be found there. Then we, after wandering miles through an unknown forest, often in the dark, may

23 King with his court officials (early thirteenth century)

find by chance some filthy hovel. Indeed, courtiers often fight for lodgings unfit for pigs.

So Peter of Blois describes the erratic behaviour of King Henry II of England, depicting the hardship and trouble caused to the royal staff when plans for travelling were changed by a ruler at the last moment. For medieval kings were usually accompanied by their court on the road.

Sometimes, when there was need for haste, a king travelled without a retinue, as in 1389 when Charles VI of France, aged about 21, wished to return quickly to Paris. He had been touring the south of France with his brother, the Duke of Touraine, accompanied by a great train. 'The town of Montpellier and its ladies afforded them much pleasure so they stayed three days there.' Then, suddenly the king flung down a challenge to his brother that he would race him to Paris, and both set off with only one attendant. They rode night and day, travelling in charettes for one stage to get some sleep. Charles took four and a half, the duke four and a third days—the king losing his wager through oversleeping at Troyes, which lapse cost him 500 francs.

24 Charles VI of France leaves Montpellier in haste

Kings often moved around their kingdoms for political reasons. They also, like all their subjects who owned more than one estate, visited each in turn to eat up its livestock and produce. Rulers and magnates had tournaments to attend at home and abroad. Wars, too, kept them on the march, pilgrimages drew them to local or distant shrines, while crusades involved long journeys to fight the infidel in the Holy Land or Egypt, in Barbary, Germany, or Spain.

*25 Richard II receives Isabella of France as his queen from
Charles VI, her father*

A king's passage through his territories caused delight to some, but despair to most of his subjects. Archbishop Islip, writing to Edward III of England stated: 'When men hear of your coming, at once for fear, they hide, or eat or get rid of their geese and chickens and other possessions, that they may not utterly lose them through your arrival.' For even a short expedition involved, in the case of an English king, not only his entire household being fed and housed, but in earlier periods the staffs of his chancery and exchequer had to be provided for as well. In addition, queens and princes sometimes accompanied the king with *their* households, and needed food and accommodation. The unfortunate officials who had to arrange for lodgings were the herbergers. In 1318 definite ordinances were drawn up regarding the allocation of lodging when the court was travelling. This stated that those members of the household

> who cannot be lodged with the king in the town must be accommodated by the herbergers 'within the verge', according to their rank . . . and those officers shall be lodged nearest to the court whose work demands proximity to it. The rest of the said household shall be as near as possible.

26 Charles IV of France enters St Denis

Peter of Blois has shown the difficulties of finding accommodation even of the poorest, so that the herbergers were sent ahead by the marshal of the household with attendant servants to find lodgings. The head carters would send staff with equipment gathered by the various departments—food, furniture, tapestries, beds, vessels for the chapel and a portable altar, carpets and mattresses, everything in fact that the king and his retinue could need.

During the fourteenth century, Chancery ceased to travel with the English king in his progresses and took up permanent quarters in Chancery Lane, London. This department of the King's court originated in the chapel when the royal chaplain and his staff wrote the king's writs. So that before about the mid-fourteenth century in England, all the Chancery personnel were liable to ride with the king when he went on progress. His archers and serjeants-at-arms also accompanied him, his serjeant of the marshalsea being at hand to help him dismount and take his horse. Bannerets, knights, esquires and yeomen were also in the king's retinue, and his physician, a confessor with a companion, and an almoner to give alms at shrines and monasteries, as well as to distribute bread, meat, ale or money to the poor, daily, also rode with him. The steward and keeper of the wardrobe had to keep accounts of expenses and present them at least every three days, even when travelling, and one or two of the king's messengers were at hand to deliver and bring back letters.

Tournaments and jousts caused royalty, magnates and knights to undertake long journeys in their own and distant countries. It is thought that these mock combats originated in France. They became very popular in England and were legalised in 1194. From about 1150 to 1350 tournaments were organised as mass meetings of side against side, which often resulted in a mêlée differing little from real war. Between 1150 and 1250 mounted knights, singly or with attendant squires, rode across Europe in search of adventure or to tourney at a combat previously arranged. Those proclaimed in France were especially famous. Combattants in a tournament ranged over a wide area of country and refuges were appointed where knights could rest and arm or disarm.

William Marshall, Earl of Pembroke (1144–1219), was often on the roads of Europe 'seeking adventure'. With his companion-at-arms, Jean d'Erlée, as renowned a minstrel as a warrior,

27 Knights and ladies ride to a tournament

William travelled for two years in France. Their adventures brought them much wealth, for in ten months alone they had captured 103 knights. Once in the Seine valley the two knights reached a certain prearranged field before their opponents. The Countess of Joigny and her ladies had come to watch the contest and were invited by the knights to dance to a song of William's. Then a young minstrel sang, his refrain being, 'Marshall give me a good horse'. At this point an opposing knight arrived and attacked William, who unhorsed him and gave his mount to the minstrel.

In William Marshall's period, knights wore a coif, or helmet of chain mail, which with a coat and leggings of chain mail completely covered the warrior from head to toe. A flat topped pot-helm was sometimes worn but was soon discarded for a pointed helm which more efficiently turned blows. Between 1250 and 1450 chain mail was strengthened by the addition of pieces of plate armour on arms and legs until by 1454 the armoured knight was completely encased in heavy plate. This cumbersome armour caused the mêlée type of tournament to be abandoned for the tournament fought in an enclosure.

In 1223 a tournament in England at Blyth, near Nottingham, drew bands of competitors from Kent, Essex, Buckinghamshire and Devon. After it, 15 barons had their lands taken into the king's hands, for these gatherings were often the pretext for baronial conspiracy or even marked the start of a rebellion. For this reason governments forbade tournaments from time to time. In 1299, for instance, when Edward I of England was fighting the Scots, 'all tourneying, seeking adventures or going with arms' was forbidden, since the king also needed all the fighting men he could get to aid him against the northern kingdom.

About 1320 the *Romance of Fulk Fitz-Warin* describes a tournament at Peveril castle.

> Then William Peverel had proclaimed in many a country and city that all brave knights who wished should tourney at castle Peverel at the feast of Michaelmass . . . the best knight to have the love of his niece Melette and be lord and master of Blancheville.

The ten sons of the duke of Little Bretagne with 100 knights attended, also Eneas, prince of Scotland with 200 knights, and the Prince of Wales also with 200, and many more.

> Garin de Mers, the Valiant went with his company and abode in tents in the forest near where the tournament should be, well clad in red samite and their horses were covered to the ground in array of war. . . . They sounded the trumpet, tabors, pipes and Saracen horns and the tourney began stiff and strong. Garin proved the most valiant and married the fair Melette there and then.

During the fourteenth century jousting or tilting between two combatants became most popular. A barrier or tilt of planks was erected and the contestants charged, one on each side, using the lance of courtesy fitted with triple points which did not penetrate armour as easily as a single point would have done. Each contestant was attended by a mounted squire. The joust master usually sat in a separate gallery, while noble spectators had another raised gallery or pavilion from which to watch. The baser sort climbed trees, or grouped themselves at some remaining vantage point.

Ladies also attended tournaments. Some who rode to a joust arranged under Edward III were described as 'not of the best of the kingdom' and roused antagonistic feelings in the more respectable.

28 The Duke of Burgundy entering Chartres with his army

They rode as if they were part of the tournament in wonderful male apparel, in parti-coloured tunics with short caps and bands wound cord-wise round their heads and girdles bound with gold and silver, and daggers in pouches at their waists. . . . These vexed their bodies with scurrilous wantonness that the murmurs of the people sounded everywhere, but they neither feared God nor blushed thereat.

Tournaments were in part a training for war, and even when actually campaigning, kings and great magnates still kept their state. When Charles the Bold of Burgundy was defeated at Nancy in 1477 by the French, his splendid tapestries were amongst the rich spoil captured from his pavilion and baggage. An earlier duke of Burgundy who commanded an expedition for his brother, Charles V of France (1364–80), is shown on a contemporary illumination entering Chartres with his army. The cavalry in elaborate armour, heralds in parti-coloured tunics and hose with banners and trumpets announce the duke's arrival at the gate; the archers also in the Burgundian livery, the horses, richly caparisoned, display the pageantry of a medieval army on the march.

Even on pilgrimage kings and magnates usually travelled with ceremony, unless it was a St Louis. Salimbene was among the brethren at the Convent of Sens when this devout king was received with all honour there. Describing him the friar writes,

> Our lord king was spare and slender . . . having the face of an angel. He came to our church not in regal pomp but in a pilgrim's habit . . . not on horseback, but on foot. Three counts followed in the same humble guise, for the king did not care for a great train of nobles but rather for the prayers of the poor.

Henry, Earl of Derby, in 1392 and Richard Beauchamp, Earl of Warwick, in 1408 undertook pilgrimages to Jerusalem. Both, however, though in pilgrim garb, travelled in state. A French writer criticises great lords for their lack of humility. When on pilgrimage or crusade 'minstrels precede them in fine purple and they feast always on the richest viands'.

29 *The Earl of Warwick starts on a pilgrimage*

An examination of the Earl of Derby's expenses' accounts during his crusading journey to Prussia in 1390 supports this criticism. The heads of various departments of his household sent servants to buy up supplies and equipment for the journey. By June the Earl's servants, horses and carts, laden with food and other necessities and with herds of live cattle for slaughtering, were traversing the roads of Lincolnshire towards Boston, to arrive at the port by 20 July. From there Henry and a few of his retinue were put ashore at Ruxhofte and travelled by cart to Putzig where a horse and saddle were bought for the Earl; later they spent a night in a roadside mill and pushed on next day to Danzig where their ship had now arrived with the rest of the household. This consisted of a chamberlain and treasurer, a clerk of the household, supervisors for stables, kitchen, buttery, pantry, poultry and falconry. There were knights, esquires and valets, many of whom had their personal servants, also a corps of bowmen, six minstrels and a trumpeter; Derby and Lancaster heralds accompanied the Earl, as well as his personal chaplain. On 16 August Henry and his retinue arrived at Konigsberg. The heavy luggage was then transferred to flat boats, other necessities went by cart to Insterburg Castle, while 22 four-horsed carts with a man, each carrying stores and baggage travelled with Derby on the campaign itself. By 21 August the train was crossing the wild frontier marches between Prussia and Lithuania. Here pack-horses were necessary to carry the baggage. On joining the crusading forces their commander, Marshal Rabe, sent his musicians to play a welcome to the earl and gifts of coursers, an ox, four sheep and two peacocks were presented.

The advance of winter halted the campaign and Derby was finally housed in a burgess' house at Danzig with some retainers, the rest after repairing a ruined mansion outside the town and building extra shacks, shivered through the icy weather until the provision of warmer garments made it more bearable. It seems that the Earl returned to England at an unrecorded date, possibly in the spring.

Fuller accounts are given of the exotic and numerous provisions that were bought for Derby's pilgrimage to Palestine in 1392. The Venetian markets were ransacked for

> live poultry with cages and food, oxen for salting, 2,250 eggs, casks
> for water, cheese, oil, potted ducks, fish, vegetables, condiments,

spices, 2,000 dates, 1,000 lb. of almonds, sweet confections and sugar, choice wines in amphorae and butts, biscuits and fresh bread, four barrels of French fruits, butter and fuel.

A lamp was hung in Derby's galley, berthed near St Nicholas' church, a special mattress, feather bed and bolster, warm clothing and a stock of kitchen-ware also went on board.

On the return journey the King of Cyprus gave the Earl a leopard which, with its keeper probably joined the menagerie at the Tower of London. He took back a Turk from Rhodes who was baptised as a Christian, and from Venice a cage specially made for the parrot—another gift—with rich furs, silks, linen, collars of silver and gilt and a chain of gold as well as a mat for the leopard. All this expenditure was met through loans from Italian merchants. In 1390 we know that Derby sent a messenger from Calais to Lombardy to borrow money from the Alberti while in 1392 the same firm lent him 8,888 ducats.

Special messengers were often entrusted with huge sums of gold. Indeed they were important members of the households of medieval rulers and magnates. Until the early twelfth century in England a special messenger service was not fully developed: the king had only one in his service. Ten or 12 messengers were, however, being sent out by the exchequer. Twice a year they were on the road with their bags of writs for the sheriffs of the various counties. They travelled on foot and at first had no special livery. They nevertheless completed their deliveries within about 15 days. Individual summonses, distraints for the king's debts or orders, regarding the conduct of treasure to London and the like, were handed to the local messenger serjeant who delivered these in person.

By the time of Richard I (1189–99), special messengers for the household were being appointed and are known to us by name— Hamelin, Lucas and Roger le Toit are among them and were probably employed by Henry II also. These messengers were paid by Chancery and in 1219 under Henry III were receiving regular wages and livery or else money with which to buy these. Robert of Germany was granted a robe of blue in that year and later others were granted a robe of russet or blue. After 1234 there were 10–15 special messengers who received regular wages, but now through the wardrobe, also shoes and robes, at first once, then later twice a year. They were all mounted, but kitchen servants, *cokini*, were sent out on foot with letters, without wearing special livery. These, under Edward II, were renamed *cursores*. Queens and princes also had their special messengers. Queen Eleanor, wife of Edward I, had two mounted messengers and five *cursores*, while Isabella, wife of Edward II had two mounted and eleven foot messengers.

The livery of the mounted messengers varied in material and style with the period. By 1296, stripes were fashionable and in that year two of Prince Edward's men Robert Manfield and Robert Rideware, were given both striped and blue material for their liveries. These colours remained fashionable for messengers' liveries throughout the fourteenth century.

Queens, who usually had fewer mounted messengers, could, however, afford to clothe them more luxuriously. In 1221 Robert le Fleming, queen's messenger, rode in a robe of brown and green trimmed with lamb's fur, while a later queen's messenger used yellow cloth and a piece of *pounacius*—a brightly coloured material—for his livery. Edward III added a lambskin to the allowance of his messengers—an indication of the improved status of this class, since the wearing of any sort of fur was regulated by law according to social position.

A fourteenth-century illustration of a mounted messenger and his groom on foot behind him shows him in a pointed hood, surmounted by a long feather, a scalloped shoulder cape, a belted tunic, buttoned in front and on the sleeves to his elbows, and tights. At his waist he carried a shield-shaped pouch embroidered with the king's arms. This together with outsize spurs were acknowledged tokens of kings' messengers. The attendant had a flat hat, wore a tunic and carried a stout staff, while at his waist was a sword and stiletto. A pouch was always given to mounted messengers on their appointment from a stock kept in the wardrobe, though in 1297

30 A fourteenth-century messenger and his groom

Robinet Little was given 2s. 'to buy him a pouch at the time when he was first made a messenger, because there was no pouch found in the wardrobe at that time'.

The usual type of pouch was of leather, strongly made. This always had the king's arms stamped or embroidered on it. On ceremonial occasions, however, a grander type, which bore the royal arms painted on it and other elaborate decorations, was used. In 1355 the Black Prince gave his favourite messenger a valuable silver-gilt box with a silver-gilt girdle 'enamelled with the ribbon' as a token of his favour. Baskets, or boxes emblazoned with the king's arms were used to carry the summons addressed to sheriffs, since pouches would have been too small.

31 A groom holds the messenger's horse and receives wine

Indeed, royal messengers, riding on the king's business, were familiar sights on medieval roads, so that Master Rypon of Durham uses the courier and his box as an illustration in one of his sermons, confident of the understanding of his listeners. The fare of English messengers was usually wholemeal bread with a 'messe of great meat', at the two meals which were customary, one at 10 a.m. and the other at 4 p.m. This was provided in the king's hall when the messenger was not travelling; when abroad on business he had money in lieu of food. Peter of Blois tells us that under Henry II messengers suffered greatly from indigestion owing to the king's unpredictable movements and

bread, hastily made, without leaven, from the dregs of the ale tub. . . . The wine is turned sour or mouldy. The ale which men drink at court is horrid to the taste and abominable to the sight. There also is such a crowd of people that sick and whole beasts are sold at random

59

with fish that is sometimes four days old; yet this corruption and stench is sold at the full price . . . and we must needs fill our bellies with carrion and our bodies become graves for sundry corpses.

A messenger was expected, however, like other members of the household to provide his own horse, nor was there compensation for its loss, even when on the king's service. Nevertheless the king sometimes granted as a favour some payment towards replacement of a horse. Edward I gave to his messenger Brehull 'thirty shillings for the replacement of his black horse, dead in parts beyond the sea'. Naturally a man took good care of his mount, riding only about three miles per hour, the pace of a foot courier and covering 20–25 miles a day. The messenger hired extra horses for an urgent journey if these were procurable. In Edward I's reign the road from London to Scotland was probably well posted as was the Dover road and that to the Welsh marches.

Carrying letters was not the sole task of messengers. They often organised and accompanied the carriage of money and valuables. Robert Manfield in 1307, for instance, had to transfer £4,000 of coinage from London to Carlisle during the Scottish war. He not only hired four carts and carters with 20 horses, but 12 men-at-arms and 16 archers as a guard, and rode with this cavalcade on the 11 days' journey to Carlisle. There, part of the gold was transferred to pack-horses, the Scottish roads being unfit for carts, and taken to Tibber's castle some 12 miles north-west of Dumfries. Manfield's bill to the wardrobe for the entire undertaking was £28 19s. 1d.

Messengers sometimes carried valuable royal gifts to various shrines. The fourteenth-century Jack Faulkes carried a golden ship from London to Our Lady of Walsingham, Edward III's thank-offering for a safe return from France.

The expenses' account of a journey to Avignon on the king's behalf by this same Faulkes supplies details of the life of these messengers while on active service. With Robert Arden, one of the *cockini* or foot-runners as his companion, Faulkes left London on 26 July 1343. He had orders to spare no expense to secure a speedy journey. One at least of the messengers was under obligation to return within 18 days 'on pain of life and limb'.

First they collected the letters from the wardrobe. These were probably under the great seal of chancery. Faulkes placed them in his emblazoned pouch then went to the exchequer to draw out £10 sterling for their expenses. Later, as the journey proved costly, he received an additional £13 10s. 4d. From the pier at Westminster they took a boat to London, bought a pair of boots and new spurs, collected their horses and rode to Dover. Next day they boarded their special barge after dinner, and spent the night at Wissant, near Calais. The 28th saw them in Paris, where they slept. They had covered 134 miles in France and must have travelled post to accomplish this in about 17 hours.

On the 29th they reached Dourdan, sent their horses back at a cost of 7d., then in order to snatch some sleep jolted on over the evil roads in a *charette* or wagon to Ouzouer-sur-Loire, near Orleans. They reached Cercy-le-Tours via Nevers by the night of the 30th after travelling another 100 miles. An early start next morning brought them to Chalons-sur-Sâone where they dined. By late afternoon they reached Lyons where they supped for 9d. This was a journey of 125 miles. If made by post horses it would have taken approximately 17 hours. In Lyons, they hired a boat for six florins of Florence and doubtless enjoyed the restful 130 mile voyage on the Rhone. They reached Avignon on 2 August 'at the hour of vespers'. After supper it was too late to deliver their letters. Did they therefore pass a convivial evening in the magnificent, corrupt and squalid city of the Popes, or did they—after their past gruelling journeys—go to bed and sleep?

Their business took five days, but Arden returned on the 8th to report to the king, riding probably to Lyons, and travelling day and night for one stage.

Faulkes left Avignon on the 12th but in Vienne was put in charge of a serjeant escort and was further delayed by having to get a letter of protection to travel through France from the French king. Medieval travellers, whether ambassadors of high rank, king's messengers or humbler folk were regarded, when foreigners, as potential spies, which indeed they often were. Even Faulkes' badge on his pouch was, on this occasion, not sufficient to take him through France without delays, so that by the 12th he had only reached Lyons and had to ride 'night and day on divers horses' from Chateauneuf to Paris. He reached Wissant on the 22nd where he slept, had a morning drink on waking and arrived in London at supper time, too late to report at court.

This was by no means the last of Faulkes' journeys for up to 1355 he travelled widely in France, Flanders and Germany and was no doubt valued as a highly experienced messenger by the king. There may have been messengers who betrayed their trust, though there is little evidence of this, but the marshal's court was empowered to deal with any officers of the household guilty of serious indiscretions. One ordinance stated:

> If any officer belonging to this court be noised as a thief or outrageous roisterer in much haunting slanderous places, company or other, then he to be rehearsed thereof afore the Sovereigns and be sent . . . to the Marshalsea prison, there to abide till he be declared, and the law will award.

The French messenger service developed on somewhat different lines from the English. Served at first by foot runners, the king, after the increase of royal power, constituted a special corps—the *chevaucheurs de l'Écurie* or Riders of the Stables. These increased in number as those of the runners diminished, so that though in 1350 there were 30 royal foot messengers, in 1380 there were only eight and in 1420 but two. On the other hand, by 1239 there were 12 *chevaucheurs* and at least 50 by 1383, without counting the 'Riders' of the Queen and princes. French conditions of service were better than those of the English messengers. Both services were provided with food or money in lieu of this, but the livery allowed to French messengers was usually of scarlet—the most highly esteemed colour in the Middle Ages—and it was embroidered with fleur-de-lys. They also received indemnity for themselves and their horses in case of accident, as well as being allowed to requisition horses when on urgent business. This led to abuses and in 1254 St Louis forbade that 'any in our kingdom should borrow a horse against the wish of the owner, if not strictly for our need'.

Most European magnates, including the dukes of Brittany and Burgundy, had special messengers in their employ from about the twelfth century. Powerful corporations, both lay and ecclesiastical, had their own private posts as had the universities and merchants of standing, such as Jacques Coeur, though only those with ample means could undertake the heavy expenses involved.

Papal messengers had even better conditions than those of other powers. Their livery was more sumptuous and their food in hall—bread, meat, fish, eggs and fruit—provided a more varied diet than English couriers, at all events, obtained. They had probably originally been chosen from the horsemen who swarmed about the papal court at Avignon. Nevertheless they proved themselves men of ability. On appointment they swore to be loyal and to give good service. In return they received a *lettere cursorie* which gave them the right to use certain ecclesiastical lodgings and to nursing care, if ill. They were later indemnified for expenses if they had forgotten to carry this letter. Horses from the papal stables were also provided for them, and if they had to buy or hire a mount they received reimbursement from the Curia.

Messengers performed other services besides carrying letters. Those too old to travel long distances at speed, became buyers for the Court. Guyot let Breton and Colin le Lombard were among these elderly couriers. One named Boloninus went to Sardinia and Campagnia to buy corn. Raymond de Béziers, from 1353–62, bought all building materials. Dominique de Lucarel travelled to Bayonne and Bordeaux for salted fish, between 1351 and 1360. Others became custodians of palaces, or took charge of important prisoners.

To augment his own small staff of messengers, the pope used the couriers of the great banking and merchant houses. But after the failure of the Bardi, Bonaccorsi and other important firms, he used the service of innkeepers to provide couriers. From 1345 to 1360 Piero de Gieri, hotelier and merchant, who also ran a postal service, became the Pope's chief outside agent for despatching letters. Piero of the Couriers, as he was called, developed a close connection with *la Scarsella*—an association of smaller Florentine traders, who ran their own messenger service. Since Piero kept his own staff of couriers and his own stable, he could always provide the Pope with a messenger, ready to leap at a moment's notice into the saddle, to gallop off with an important letter. No financial problem caused delay, since Piero's account was regularly settled at intervals with the Curia.

To Piero's inn came messengers of papal legates and of leading commercial houses. In the great hall after supper, their saddle bags emptied of official letters safely delivered, their riding boots pulled off, the messengers exchanged news and stories of the lands and cities they had visited. The Curia itself was avid for news, and through Piero's most dependable messengers he built up an information agency so valuable that, at the end of 1355, his nephew was appointed to organise the intelligence service of the legates of Aquitaine, travelling with them and a staff of messengers through the district of Carcassonne. His expenses were later paid by the Curia.

It is not known whether other postal organisations as important as Piero's were carried on from Avignon. He was succeeded by Tommaso Cardini as 'master of the post', whose organisation was also used by the papacy. Nor is it known whether independent organisations provided for their couriers in sickness or old age. In England, messengers received pensions or direct alms, a sinecure post or a corrody—the right to food and shelter, when old, at a religious house. France and the Curia also provided for their aged servants of the post. Although, therefore, a messenger's life was hard, it was varied and interesting, and was sometimes rewarded by the friendship of kings, princes and the magnates they served. More important, perhaps, provided they performed their duties conscientiously, they were assured of care and security in sickness and old age.

5

Soldiers and free companies

Since war was both endemic and epidemic in the Middle Ages, never a year went by when armed men were not marching to skirmish or to battle, somewhere on the roads of Christendom. *The Song of Roland* presents as vividly as a coloured motion picture, or as if we watched from a tournament gallery, the spectacle of an eleventh century host passing by in all its splendour. Individuals, too, are graphically presented, as if we saw them face to face. Here is the young knight, Roland, gallant and impetuous, riding out to his last encounter:

> *Through Gate of Spain goes Roland riding past*
> *On Veillantif, his swiftly running barbe;*
> *Well it becomes him to go equipped in arms,*
> *Bravely he goes and tosses up his lance,*
> *High in the sky he lifts his lancehead far,*
> *A milk white pennon is fixed upon the shaft,*
> *Whose falling fringes whip his hand on the haft,*
> *Nobly he bears him, with open face he laughs.*

32 Knights of c. 1096 when the 'Song of Roland' was written

The Saracen army is also seen as it advanced against Roland and Oliver. Although the date of the battle is 15 August 778, the *Song* in the form we have it was written around the year 1096, so that Christian and Saracen knights are described as wearing armour known to the poet. This is also depicted on the contemporary Bayeux tapestry: pointed helms with protective nasals worn over hoods of chain mail; tunics of chain mail protecting the entire body to below the knees, while the knights carried almond shaped shields, lances, swords and battle-axes.

As the vast host of Saracens advanced, it struck dismay into Oliver as he reconnoitred from a hilly crest.

> *Now are the paynims in Sarsen hauberks dight*
> *Whereof the most with triple mail are lined;*
> *Good Saragossa helms they lace on tight,*
> *Swords of Viana steel gird on their thighs;*
> *Spears of Valence they have and shields full fine,*
> *Their gonfalons are scarlet, blue and white.*
> *They leave their mules, their palfreys leave behind,*
> *And mount their steeds, in serried ranks they ride.*

At this time and for some time to come the armies of Christendom were feudal in character. Their main strength consisted of landed magnates and their tenants who owed military service to their lords and to the king, in return for the lands they held of them. Magnates also had a bodyguard of household retainers, engaged for long periods, or for life. These moved with their lord and were often bound to him by bonds of friendship in addition to that imposed by their oath of loyalty. The service owed to the king by the lords and their knightly tenants, was however, limited in duration and had to be supplemented in time of need by that of paid mercenaries. Finally, these cavalry forces—paid and feudal—were combined with infantry, armed with bows or lances, serving, irrespective of tenure, as an obligation of their allegiance.

By the time of Froissart, paid armed forces serving under contract were taking the place of feudal levies, although as yet no standing regular army was employed by any European ruler. The English, according to Froissart, would never go on campaign without strong financial inducements. When Pope Urban VI offered, during the period of the papal schism, absolution from all crimes and faults to those who would help to destroy the supporters of his rival Clement, Froissart stated:

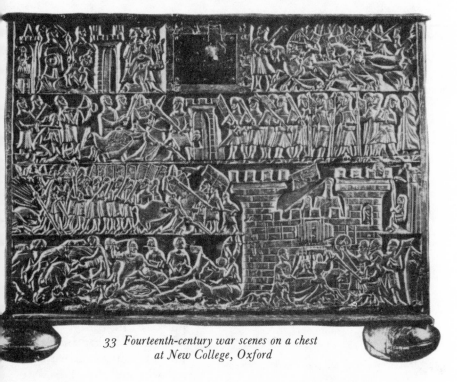

*33 Fourteenth-century war scenes on a chest
at New College, Oxford*

It was well known that the nobles of England, for all the absolutions in the world, would undertake no expedition unless it was preceded by offers of money. Men-at-arms cannot live upon pardons and, it is to be feared, they do not value them greatly except at the point of death.

The costly show and equipment put on by magnates when marching to battle had all to be paid for, and by the fourteenth and fifteenth centuries the passion for blazonry, tournaments and courtly romance, and all the trappings of the orders of chivalry, had become a façade which disguised, to some extent, the materialistic and commercial character of later medieval warfare. Froissart presents us with the French army approaching the town of Bourbourg in 1383:

As they approached the town, the French lords made a splendid show; banners and pennons were flying in the wind, each lord arranged with his own men beneath his banner. The Lord de Coucy and his state were particularly outstanding. Mounted on a beautiful

67

*34 Armed knight of the fourteenth century—
symbol of King Robert of Sicily*

horse, he rode from side to side before his men, addressing them in a most agreeable manner. . . . He had moreover, led coursers, richly caparisoned and ornamented with housings, with the ancient arms of Coucy mixed with those he now bore. Other great lords also kept up a state suitable to their dignity, and on this day more than four hundred knights were created.

The chronicler has succeeded in introducing into his description of an English army on the march, a much more practical and business-like note. In the winter of 1356, after the Black Prince's victory at Poitiers, Edward III left Rheims:

As Edward marched with his immense army towards Paris, his marshals and light troops scoured the country around, burning and destroying it, but frequently bringing in provision for the army.

I must inform you that the king of England and his rich lords were followed by carts laden with tents and pavilions, mills to grind their corn, and forges to make shoes for their horses. These carts were six thousand in number, each drawn by four strong horses which had been brought from England.

Even in the most idealistic periods, war had always been regarded as a game of chance in which the prizes were the huge ransoms which could be demanded from prisoners of wealth and note, the seizure of costly booty, or the winning of fame, of favours or a knighthood from their prince. Every aspect of medieval warfare had its own rules, which though by no means always followed, at least set a standard as to conduct. Every marching army knew that a 'law of arms' existed—at least during the later Middle Ages. Every soldier was aware of an ideal standard of military conduct which he was called upon to honour. The majority probably had no intention of doing so, but the very fact of a law of arms, supported by courts specially appointed to try breaches of its regulations, to which those with a grievance might appeal, must have acted as a curb on the unruly. In England, there was the Court of Chivalry where the Lord High Constable and the Earl Marshal presided as judges in the White Chamber at Westminster. In France, there were the Courts of the Constable held in the Table de Marbre in Paris. The Dukes of Burgundy, of Anjou and of Brittany, all had their courts where the law of arms was administered, and there were many lesser tribunals to which cases of dispute over ransoms, over wrongful imprisonment during or after a campaign, or over loss of booty and so on could be tried.

In many respects the law of arms was related to the rules of the cult of chivalry and both remained as a background to all the warfare of the Middle Ages. The laws of chivalry were universally known and held as universally binding. Princes and men-at-arms

35 Fighting at Brest during the Hundred Years War

alike were bound by them and became equals in law before them. One of their tenets was that faith must be kept, even with the enemy.

In 1418 a French captain, Jean d'Angennes, might have been met travelling fast from Cherbourg towards Rouen. He was happy in the fact that he had money in his pouch and also a safe conduct granted by the English. He had just negotiated the surrender of Cherbourg and was rewarded by his enemies for this. Later, however, he was captured in Rouen by Henry V and was put on trial 'for taking money for the surrender of Cherbourg while it was still stuffed with supplies and artillery'. This was against the regulations of the law of arms. Jean, a Frenchman, was convicted and executed by the English for a crime which had been to their advantage. Henry V, acting as a knight, not as a foreign king, was 'keeping faith, even with the enemy' by punishing a transgressor against the chivalric laws—binding on all soldiers of Christendom.

According to the law of arms war could only be legally waged at all when it was 'just'. Lawyers defined this as one instigated by the authority of a ruler who 'administered high and low justice'. Only during a just war was incendiarism, pillaging, killing and the ransom of prisoners legal.

By the law of arms all loot belonged to the leader of battle. Soldiers were supposed to carry all they had plundered to some central place where it was sold and the proceeds divided among the combatants, according to their rank. A percentage of the booty and of ransoms had to go to the prince. This varied in different countries—in England it was a third, in Spain a fifth and in France was exacted from booty worth under 10,000 francs.

There were often disputes concerning prisoners. During the battle of Neville's Cross in 1346, for instance, between Scots and English, Ralph de Bethom captured a certain John of Niddesdale. Now the king had ordered all prisoners to be taken to London where the council would treat with their captors concerning them. De Bethom, however, rode home with John and imprisoned him in a lonely peel tower in Westmorland, probably intending to negotiate secretly for his ransom. The story, told in the Patent Rolls, continues:

The king now learns that Ralph de Bethom . . . would have brought John of Niddesdale to London, but Thomas de Ros of Kendal Castle

*36 1377, a French castle besieged by mercenaries under Owen of Wales,
who is shown on the right, treacherously killed by one of his men*

with his brother and others, took the said prisoner out of custody at
Haverbrack and returned him to Scotland for a ransome of 500£,
in contempt of the king and to his damage by 1000£.

A commission was set up in the north to deal with the case.

Although the law of arms aimed at keeping aggression during
a war within legal bounds, these attempts were frustrated by the
illegal activities of the Free Companies, who ranged far and
wide during periods of truce and of peace, as freebooters in
Spain, Navarre, France, Germany and the Italian states. It was
inevitable that these companies should be formed during a
period when there were no regular paid standing armies. These
unemployed soldiers were willing to travel anywhere to fight,
provided they were offered enough money and the chance to
win booty. Froissart describes them after the Peace of Bretigny,
in 1360, which ended the first phase of the Hundred Years War:

71

Many disbanded soldiers, having been long accustomed to pillage, were loth to give up their mode of life. They banded themselves together, chose leaders, and at length, collected in several companies, made their stand in Burgundy and Champagne; they scoured the countryside and captured the fort of Joinville, taking 100,000 francs which they divided among themselves. By Lent they numbered 16,000 men. . . . At last, the Marquis de Montferrat, who was at war with the Lords of Milan, divided 60,000 florins among them and by offering them high pay, led them to fight in Lombardy.

At times, the Free Companies succeeded in taking a town without violence. This was usually when they resorted to stratagem. A young squire, captain of a company, told Froissart a story concerning such a capture one Christmastide when they were lodged in the same hotel. It has a delightful fairy tale atmosphere which suited the season:

I will tell you how I captured the castle and town of Thurie in the Albigeois . . . said the squire. Near the town is a beautiful spring from which, each morning, the women of the town draw water. So, taking fifty men with me, we rode all day over heaths and through forests until about midnight I placed an ambuscade near Thurie. Myself, with six others, disguised as women with pails on our heads, hid in haycocks near the town. As it was the season round St John's Eve the haygrass had been cut. The hour for opening the gates at last arrived. The women came to the fountain; then each of us also filled his pail and made for the town . . . where only an old cobbler kept the gate.

One of the party blew his horn, the companies in ambuscade at once joined the 'water-women' and all entered the town. In this way it passed quietly into their hands.

But the majority of the Free Companies' exploits were far from being free from violence. Salimbene described the sufferings of the Italian peasants in the thirteenth century:

Villagers were wont to dwell apart, nor did they resist their enemies. One night the soldiery burned fifty three houses in the village and only stopped for the prayers of the Friars Minor. The men of Bibbiano gave £100 imperial to the men of Gesso and made a truce with them for one year that they might gather their harvests in safety. The men of Castelli carried away and rebuilt their houses on the summit of Mt. Bianello. . . . But the men of San Polo d'Enza built houses round the church, then dug moats and filled them with water that they might be protected. Nevertheless many were killed working in their fields. One who defended his oxen was slain. His fellow they beat and left for dead.

The *Assempri* of Fra Filippo in the fourteenth century and the sermons of S. Bernadino in the fifteenth, record even worse excesses. Fra Filippo relates how, at the sack of Faenza the famous condottiere Sir John Hawkwood, whose equestrian portrait is in the cathedral of Florence, stabbed a young nun at her prayers. Yet Hawkwood was a knight and bound by his vows to respect the laws of war which expressly made the religious, pilgrims and hermits, and oxherds and ploughmen, immune from warlike aggression. Honoré Bonet stated in his *Tree of Battle*:

> Those who cultivate the soil, plough and work for everybody, and all manner of folk live by their labour.

Then, he adds callously,

> If sometimes the humble and innocent suffer harm and lose their goods, it cannot be otherwise.

37 Sepulchral monument of Sir John Hawkwood in Florence Cathedral

Sometimes during their travels these *écorcheurs* or *scorchers* met with a fate they well deserved. In 1446 two men-at-arms of the company of Rodriguo de Villandro one of the *écorcheurs* of the Duke of Bourbon, who had perpetrated many crimes in the district, demanded lodging at the inn of one Antoine. They promised to pay for all they consumed and after supper retired to sleep in the stable where their horses were housed. Antoine and four friends determined to take vengeance on the soldiers, who were seized, bound,

38 Execution of Sylvester Budes

taken into the forest and murdered. The peasants sold their victims' horses in Vienne for nine good honest crowns. Fearing discovery, however, all five men left the district. They were later apprehended and at their trial it was found that

they had acted only after unendurable pillaging had almost ruined them, after ransoms had drained them dry and looting had emptied their homes. In addition their village had been attacked and its people beleagured in the church by armed men. . . . In other things the accused are of good fame . . . we have granted them pardon.

The whirligig of time brought its deserved revenges to another notorious condottiere, Sylvester Budes. He had marched against Pope Urban VI and was defeated and captured by Sir John Hawkwood. Escaping, he took refuge with the rival pope, Clement VI. Unfortunately for Budes the Cardinal of Amiens, whom the free-booter had once robbed, was staying with Clement. He advised the Pope to put Budes to death. An illumination in Froissart's *Chronicles* shows Budes kneeling in his armour. A mere page boy is about to strike off his head while Pope and Cardinal stand nonchalantly with their backs to the scene.

It is difficult to find anywhere in the records a favourable comment on the Free Companies in the Middle Ages. But Friar Felix Fabri, returning from his first pilgrimage, stopped with four companions at an inn for the night. On hearing that some armed knights of the Duke of Austria were expected, the four pilgrims moved on, declaring it was unsafe to dwell with men-at-arms. Fabri, however, stayed, and wrote:

Soon the inn was full of these fierce men. But when they heard I had visited the Holy Land they asked me to say mass on the morrow and travel with them. I did so and breakfasted with them. Then they paid my bill and took me with them in pleasant comfort.

On overtaking the other pilgrims Felix found they had been beaten, robbed and wounded by robbers on their way. 'I was very sorry for my brethren', wrote Felix, 'but also glad I had not been of their company.'

Nevertheless, the consensus of opinion from non-combatants would support the verdict of the four medieval pilgrims 'that it was unsafe to dwell with men-at-arms'. Roads were rendered dangerous by them to travellers, fairs could not be held, craftsmen and traders could not pursue their livelihood, nor peasants cultivate their fields, monks had to flee from monasteries and a contemporary poet put into words the feeling of all these persecuted people:

> *So were it goodè at this tide*
> *That every man upon this side*
> *Besought and prayèd for the peace*
> *Which is the cause of all increase*
> *Of worship and of worldès wealth*
> *Of heartès good and soulès health.*
> *Withouten peace stands nothing good;*
> *Therefore to Christ who shed His blood*
> *For peace, beseek peace for all men.*
> *Amen, amen, amen, amen.*

6

Outlaws and vagabonds

The legal definition of the word 'outlaw' implies the overriding conditions of his life. He was essentially a fugitive from justice who by refusing to submit to trial put himself—by a legal decision of one of the king's courts—'outside the law'. He was declared a *wargus* (Old Norse *wargr*, a wolf, is one suggested derivation of the word). He became a hunted creature with the price of a wolf set on his head—indeed, his 'wolf's head' was proclaimed about the country. All were ordered to capture him if possible, though it was a felony to kill him. His goods were forfeit, his revenues temporarily in the king's hand, though he could reclaim his rightful inheritance if pardoned. Some outlaws had a sentence of banishment imposed. These were forced to wander abroad as exiles.

Outlaws were most numerous during the periods when the central government was weak. In fact, the imposition of a sentence of outlawry was a confession that those in authority had failed to bring a criminal to justice and so to impose law and order upon him. It might also imply that the integrity of judges and of justice itself was in doubt—that it was preferable to escape to the wilds rather than submit to its doubtful decisions.

Yet many outlaws, during the Middle Ages and after, became folk-heroes. The English Hereward the Wake and Fulk Fitz-warin, the Scottish William Wallace and Murray of Ettrick, the French Eustace the Monk are among historical characters who were outlawed. To their actual exploits fabulous deeds were added, and these, turned into story, folk song and ballad, were recited and sung in castle hall and taverns. The historicity of the even more popular Robin Hood has not yet been proved, though likely candidates have been found during the thirteenth and fourteenth centuries.

Two characteristics are common to all the outlaw stories. Each of the heroes is resisting oppression, and all are shown as aiding the poor or unfortunate. Hereward the Wake makes himself the spearhead against the tyrannous Norman conquerors of the English; Fulk Fitzwarin resists the despotic king John, Eustace the Monk fights the injustice of his overlord the count of Boulogne; while Robin Hood wages continuous war against the representatives of injustice and avarice in church and state—the iniquitous sheriff of Nottingham and the grasping abbots, friars and monks who ride in state about the countryside.

39 *Robin Hood and Little John*

From these legendary accounts, true pictures of the everyday life of outlaws and of the social conditions of their periods can be drawn. They mirror very closely the accounts in the records. Many outlaws are described as making long journeys abroad as well as in their own countries. Their habitat is the forest, moor or mountain. They must live on what they can catch and hunt. The chronicle *Gesta Herewardi*, the *Deeds of Hereward*, gives a vivid account of how these Saxon rebels lived in the monastery of Ely, in the fastnesses of the Fens.

These men are desperate, a certain Deda told king William. They are prepared for attack at any moment. All dine together, monk and soldier, each with his arms hung by him on the walls, ready to be seized at a moments notice. The Abbot and earls dine at high table with Hereward and other leading outlaws. They have erected strong defences. All help to till the soil, though they could live by hunting alone. The waters abound in fish, the woods in wild beasts and heron. A thousand birds can be taken at one time from a single marsh.

A thirteenth-century chronicle describes other Saxon outlaws who established sporadic pockets of resistance against the Normans' cruel forest laws. They were protesting against the destruction of villages and cultivated lands to make hunting grounds.

Those of the English who were of gentle birth were driven from their lands. . . . With their kindred they took refuge in the woods, living by what they could hunt. From their lairs and waste places they laid a thousand ambushes and traps for the Normans.

To gain food at all, outlaws were forced to break the forest laws imposed with such savage punishments by the Normans. This alone made them heroes in the eyes of the common man. Between foresters and outlaws there existed, therefore, the bitterest enmity. Robin Hood on a journey to Nottingham is described as killing 15—this with the obvious approval of the writer of the ballads who lived in the fifteenth century, when the law of venison was still in operation.

The way of life of the outlaw of the ballad also mirrors contemporary discontents, especially in his bitterest enmities. Robin Hood's hatred of extortionate churchmen, corrupt sheriffs and justices echoes that of the English people as a whole. Sir Richard atte Lee, an impoverished knight in debt to the Abbot of St Mary's, York, is befriended by Robin Hood. When the knight begged for time to pay and retrieve his land, we are told

> *The abbot sware a full great oath*
> *By God that died on tree,*
> *'Get thee land where thou may*
> *For thou gettest none of me.'*

It was because of such heartless extortions as this that Robin Hood ordered his followers to 'beat and bind' all evil-living clerics. On the other hand he is represented as without enmity to the Church itself and its services. It was against corrupt ecclesiastics that he warred.

> *Yet one thing grieves me, said Robin*
> *And does my heart much woe,*
> *That I may not, no solemn day*
> *To mass or matins go.*

Neither is Robin shown as being antagonistic to the hierarchical organisation of society. He is loyal to his King.

I love no man in all the world
So well as I do my king.

he declares. Indeed he believes that the various orders of society should keep their due state and is shocked that the knight Sir Richard atte Lee has not even a squire to attend him.

It were great shame said Robin
A knight alone to ride.

So Little John is provided to accompany the knight as his escort.

Robin Hood himself is the captain of his band and like the retainers of magnates and landed gentry his followers wear his livery as did the men of the Scottish outlaw Murray.

His merrie men are in livery clad
Of the Lincoln green so fair to see.

It was essential, of course, for all retainers to be trained in the use of weapons. To outlaws, skill at archery was especially important, both for killing game and for defending themselves. Robin Hood and his men are portrayed as excelling in this.

Little John and good Scathelock
Were archers good and free
Little Much and good Reynold
The worst they would not be.

But Robin was their champion shot.

Thrice Robin shot about
And always sliced the wand.

Approving of the social order as they did, outlaws are not portrayed in ballads and stories as being antagonistic to Law in itself, but only as taking it into their own hands when they considered that justice had been perverted through the influence or action of some powerful magnate or sheriff. In 1336 a historical outlaw who called himself 'Lionel, king of the rout of raveners' wrote a letter (which has happily survived) from 'our Castle of the North wind in the Green Tower, in the first year of our reign to Richard Snaweshill, chaplain of Huntington, near York:

40 Execution in Paris of Aymerigot Marcel, an outlawed knight who had terrorized Auvergne in the fourteenth century

We command you, on pain to lose all that can stand forfeit against our laws, that you immediately remove from office him whom you maintain in the vicarage of Burton Agnes; and that you suffer that the Abbot of St Mary's have his right in this matter, and that the election of the man whom he has chosen, who is more worthy of advancement than any of your lineage, be upheld. And if you do not do this we make our vow, first to God, and then to the King of England and to our crown, that you shall have such treatment at our hands as the Bishop of Exeter had in Cheep (1326. Bishop Stapledon murdered there.). And we shall hunt you down, even if we come to Coney Street in York to do it. And show this letter to your lord, and bid him to cease from false compacts and confederacies and to suffer right to be done to him whom the Abbot has presented; else he shall have a thousand pounds worth of damage by us and our men. And if you do not take cognizance of our orders we have bidden our lieutenant in the north to levy such great distraint upon you as is spoken of above.

Several points in the letter bring out what is characteristic of many outlaws. The outlaw Lionel is a king of his rout. He wears a crown, demands allegiance and has his own Lieutenant of the North to obey his commands, but he claims his kingship under God and the King of England. Although an outlaw, he is loyal still to his faith and to his ruler. Lionel also believes that his candidate for the office of Vicar of Burton Agnes is more worthy of the post than the man Richard Snaweshill has appointed. Moreover it is clear that it is Richard's lord who is behind the opposition to the Abbot of St Mary's. It is not only Richard who is threatened, who will be hunted down if he fails to obey Lionel, but the magnate supporting him will have a thousand pounds worth of damage done to his property also, if he continues to oppose the Abbot of St Mary's. Lionel believes in the justice of his actions and this lies behind much of the violence of the outlaws. In an age when justice could not be gained through the rightful channels, especially against a magnate, the only recourse was to take the law into their own hands. So that the journeys of these men along the roads armed as if for war would seem at least sometimes justified. They were, after all, only imitating the magnate and his retainers by so doing.

Later in the fourteenth century a family of outlaws, the Beckwiths of Beckwithshawe near Harrogate, led a violent revolt at the time when the northern counties and that of the County Palatine of Chester rose in protest, proclaiming that John of Gaunt was threatening their liberties. The Beckwiths and their confederates were accused by one of Gaunt's officers of

committing wrongs and alliances that they had ordained at their parliament called 'Dodelowe' held at divers times of the year in the subversion of law, oppression of the people and disinherison of the said duke. They came armed against the castle of Haywra (Haverah) destroyed the park and did mischief in the Forest of Knaresborough.

Here the Beckwiths have not claimed that they wear a crown but have set up their own Parliament which met regularly, framed its own laws and proclaimed alliances. It is significant that this was what Lionel accused his magnate opponent of doing of 'making

41 Sir William Stapleton of Cumberland, outlawed in 1444

false compacts and alliances'. These of the Beckwiths appear to have been counter-alliances to those of John of Gaunt, a royal duke. But the Beckwiths performed what Lionel had merely threatened. They did 'a thousand pounds' worth of damage' against Gaunt's castles, parks and forests and broke down the fences of the park at 'Haywra'. Like the ballad hero Adam Bell,

They broke his parks and slew his deer
Overall they chose the best
Such peerless outlaws as they were
Walked not by east or west.

It cannot be claimed, however, as the ballads appear to do, that all outlaws were 'peerless' sheep in wolves' clothing. Many historic outlaws deserved the epithet of having 'wolves' heads' and merited the fate that was meted out to these savage beasts. Sir William Stapleton of Edenhall, Cumberland, was an example of the ruthless outlaw whose acquisitive and violent deeds forced him finally to take to the fells to escape justice. After his father's death he began a feud against his step-mother Mary, who through her husband's will had acquired many of the Stapleton manors. William, in his attempts to wrest these from her, was constantly to be seen on the road at the head of his retainers with various landowners who supported him; he took possession of manors and lands that were Mary's, waylaid and robbed her brother-in-law's servant as he rode to hand over several of her charters and deeds, burned Stapleton woods in order to lay the blame on his step-mother and even took by force from the under-sheriff a writ concerning an inquisition about the case, in order to alter the wording of the verdict given, to his own advantage. The quarrel was pursued for twelve years (1432–44). When finally the king's serjeant-at-law came to arrest Stapleton 'he could not be found, having fled to places unknown to escape arrest'. William was an outlaw motivated apparently by self-interest, without any of the saving graces of a Beckwith or of a Lionel 'king of the rout of raveners'.

Nevertheless, even here, it was the failure of the régime to keep order and give impartial justice which produced the outlaw. The same can be claimed for the vagabond of medieval times. There is indeed a logical connection between the *argus* or outlaw and the vagabond or *vagus* mentioned in many laws.

After the Norman conquest vagabondage increased, due largely to the fact that many men who had previously been free became bondmen, while those of higher rank, deprived of their lands, took to the wilds as we have seen, defied the government and became outlaws. The law attempted to prevent the bondman from escaping from his overlord and following a nomadic life.

> Bondmen shall not leave their lands nor scheme how to defraud their lord of the services due to him; and if any bondman so depart a man shall not harbour him or his goods but shall cause him to return to his lord with all that is his.

One way in which these wanderers made a living was to rob churches and despoil graves. They went sometimes from country

42 An outlaw claims the sanctuary of an abbey

to country and the Anglo Saxon chronicle in 1102 describes a descent of foreign vagabonds on England.

> In this year . . . there came thieves from Auvergne from France and Flanders. They broke into the minster of Peterborough and seized gold and silver roods, chalices and candlesticks.

Such wandering law-breakers were difficult to bring to justice, especially as they often received hospitality and protection, giving their services to their host and sometimes their stolen goods in return for better terms of service. It was therefore frequently in vain that a law of 1166 decreed:

> Let there be none in city, borough or castle who shall forbid the sheriff to enter their land or take any accused—robbers, murderers, receivers of such or outlawed, or accused with regard to the forest. The King bids them aid in capturing such men.

It was also forbidden to entertain either friend or stranger for longer than two nights, during which time the host was held responsible for his guest's behaviour, and from the third day for making good any injury inflicted by a guest who was unable or unwilling to pay his own fine or dues. Rather than risk being handed over to the sheriff or returned to an oppressive serfdom, fugitives became vagrants or joined a band of outlaws in the forest. For if they succeeded in evading capture for a year and a day then one of the Conqueror's laws declared: 'from that day they shall be free and remain free for ever.'

43 A crippled vagabond

Vagabonds largely made up the crowd of beggars which waited at the gates of monasteries, castles and manor houses for the doles of food that were put out daily. These consisted of thick *trenchers* of bread—slices cut thick and used in lieu of plates. Meat and gravy was placed on them and, if the trencher were not eaten, it went into the alms dish which was later put out for the poor. Rich men like Sir Hugh Mortimer of

Cleobury often left bequests to benefit the poor and homeless. On the anniversary of Hugh's death

> a hundred poor persons were plentifully fed, each having a loaf and two herrings because the anniversary fell in Lent. Each day in the hostelry he established, beggars and strangers received charities which no man could number.

But as the Middle Ages progressed the lot of the vagabond and poor became harder. By 1272 laws against them became stricter and they were forced to keep to the forest or open country. Strangers entering towns were arrested and kept until morning, unless they could produce bona fide credentials. It was decreed:

> If no suspicion be found he shall go quit. But if they find cause of suspicion they shall deliver him to the sheriff, who shall keep him safely until he shall be delivered in due manner.

The lot of the transgressor was certainly hard.

The scourge of the Black Death in the mid-fourteenth century caused an increase of vagrancy. Since labour was difficult to come by, workers were able to demand higher wages, which, if not given on the manor where they had been born, caused them to take to the road and to stop only where they could labour on their own terms. Legislation failed to stop the wanderings of workers and their claim for higher wages. It was now forbidden even to give alms to vagrants.

> Many valient (able-bodied) beggars refuse to labour. Since they can live by begging and give themselves to idleness and vice, to theft and other abominations, none under pain of imprisonment shall through pity give alms to such, so that thereby they shall be compelled to labour for their living.

Similar laws were promulgated in most countries of Europe. About 1363 Nuremburg and Colmar in Germany made rules forbidding the 'valiant' to beg. Those who refused had their names enrolled in a book and had to wear a special badge, a regulation which became almost universal. A licence to beg, renewable every six months, had to be obtained. Beggars might 'sing out for alms' as they travelled the road, but silence was compulsory when they stood still or sat, a device perhaps to keep them moving.

The church still taught, however, that it was a virtue to give alms and Richard Rolle of Hampole near Doncaster, a hermit of the order of St Augustine who died in 1378, wrote:

> *When thou mayest help through wisdom and skill*
> *And will not help but holdest thee still:*
> *When thou speakest sharply to the poor*
> *That some good ask at thy door*
> *Be it without, be it within,*
> *Yet it is a venial sin.*

The poor, especially those who were maimed or blind, frequently begged at shrines, sure of alms from the devout. Medieval beggars were often revolting sights through disease, or through self-inflicted cruelties or from savage punishments and vengeance. A favourite stance of these supplicants was at crosses erected on the highways, or at the intersection of roads, and the saying 'to beg like a cripple at a cross' was coined during this period. Another adage, 'I know you as well as the beggar knows his dish', comes from the mendicants' use of a clack-dish. This was an alms-basket or bowl with a clapper—compulsory for lepers, who were compelled to keep their distance when begging. Other beggars also found it useful to use a clapper to attract attention.

In periods of truce or peace during the Hundred Years War swarms of soldiers were without employment in England and France. These swelled the ranks of sturdy beggars and many found it profitable to claim that they were 'home from the wars' whether this was true or not. In England a law was passed in 1376 to deal with this problem and forbade:

> Any Robertsman or ruffian to make themselves gentlemen or men-at-arms or archers. If they cannot prove themselves so, let them be driven to their occupation or service or place from whence they came.

But the practice of claiming to have fallen from some higher or more romantic estate remained, since it proved a profitable type of appeal, and in the sixteenth century Audeley states:

> These kind of *vacabondes* will go commonly well apparelled without any weapon and in places where they meet together as at their hostelries they will bear the port of right good gentlemen. . . . Yet commonly they will steal a pair of sheets or a coverlet before the master or dame be stirring.

Many medieval beggars became staff-strikers, cudgel players or quarterstaff men and wandered in parties from village to village as entertainers. But the greater number became sturdy rogues and robbers. Laws were made in most countries at this time making imprisonment the penalty for refusing work.

Nevertheless, Langland's compassion for the poor typifies a growing concern for the miseries of the indigent in winter compelled to

> go wet-shod, frost-bitten with blains on their fingers besides being foully reviled by the rich which is pitiful to hear. Oh Lord! send a summer of comfort and joy at length to them who have spent their lives in such want and misery.

Indeed even more progressive was the idea that the lot of the worker and of the poor should be bettered in this life, and not left for the uncertainties of a life to come. By an Act of the English Parliament at Cambridge in 1388 servants were allowed to leave their work and wander in search of new employment, provided they carried letters testimonial from the duly appointed authorities of their district. This act also differentiated between the able beggar and the aged or impotent. Concerning the latter, it was decreed that they should remain in the town where they were living at the time of the proclamation of the Statute, unless that town was unable to provide for them, when they were to return to their native place which must support them. This Act has been called the first English Poor Law since the upkeep of the impotent poor was made incumbent on a township. But up to the fifteenth century imprisonment remained the punishment for wandering and begging, and many so apprehended were left so long in the ghastly conditions of a medieval prison that hundreds died. In 1495 therefore it was ordained:

> That all idle vagabonds living suspiciously shall be set in the stocks for three days and nights on bread and water; thereafter they shall avoid the town, but if taken again in the same place, shall sit in the stocks for six days and nights with the same diet. Any aiding or feeding them shall forfeit 12d. for each offence.

Nevertheless charity was still being given to beggars and at the burial of the Duke of Buckingham who was beheaded in 1521 an eye-witness stated:

There was such a number of beggars that might lie or stand about the Duke's house that a great barn was prepared for them and a fat ox was boiled with furmenty for them with bread and drink in abundance; and every person had two pence, for such was the dole. At night the beggars remained in the barn, seven score of them, every one with his woman. Thus burial was turned to boosing, mourning to mirth, fasting to feasting and lamenting to lechery.

In the sixteenth century the parson William Harrison describing the vagabonds of his time shows that they had changed little during the centuries.

What notable robbings and pilferings, murders, rapes and stealing of young children who were burned and their limbs broken to make them pitiful in people's eyes. But, for their idle *rogin* about the country the law ordains correction.

This was arrest and trial. If guilty of vagabondage the culprit was burned with a hot iron through the lobe of his right ear. Nevertheless attempts were being made throughout Europe to legislate in aid of impotent beggars and for the aged and ailing poor. The emergence of a world based on competition had caused a rapid increase in the number of destitute; able-bodied men and women were homeless and wandering the roads in 'intolerable swarms'. It was still a crime to be workless while to aid them

44 A maimed beggar

incurred fines or punishment. In 1529 Nottingham indicted several civic officials 'for suffering valiant beggars'.

Nevertheless by 1523 Luther and in 1526 the great educationalist and humanist Vives were writing in support of aid to the poor. The latter drew up a scheme for aiding the destitute in Bruges and wrote:

> It should be the task of a city's governor to strive that one man should aid another . . . that the stronger should stand by the weaker. And just as in a wealthy home it were a disgrace for the father thereof to allow any to go naked, hungry or in rags, so in a city, magistrates should not allow any citizen to suffer hunger and poverty.

This change of attitude was bound to affect the life of at least some vagabonds, if only to draw them off the roads to towns where poor relief was offered.

7

Wandering entertainers

Jongleurs, joculares, and *joculatores* are not mentioned in the Latin documents of the clerks before the ninth century. Who and what were they? The jongleur can be described as combining the functions of a musician, a poet, an actor and a mountebank; he was the entertainer *par excellence* at royal courts, and as the leader of a royal company himself held the title of king or of marshal. Yet he could be a vagabond tramping the roads and playing to country folk on the village green and at fairs. He sang *gestes* to pilgrims, he was both author and actor of many of the plays staged at the church door, which were often in competition with those performed in and by the church. He was fiddler and master of the dance whose music set youths dancing and carolling. He, in company with others banged the tabor, sounded the trumpet and beat the drum at the head of processions. At feasts, weddings and vigils he told stories, sang ballads and droned out dirges.

45 A juggler, musician and female tumbler

He was acrobat, juggler and tight-rope walker; he ate fire and swallowed swords, he performed with animals he had trained and mimed and made coarse jokes. Yet to describe him in such wholesale fashion is to combine the jongleur of all periods and give a false impression. For in character, skills and repertoire the jongleur varied from period to period, and one of the fraternity of the fifteenth century would probably have been disowned with contempt by the gleeman of the eleventh.

During this latter century, when Europe was still in a state of siege, when the warlike duchy of Normandy and the County of Anjou were at the height of their powers, when the organisation of society was feudal, the relationship of a man to his lord, to his group and to his comrade-in-arms was paramount. Loyalty and courage in battle were the highest virtues and the influence of women, the emotions of romantic love and of chivalry were generally, until towards the end of the century, undeveloped.

It was for this essentially man's world that poets wrote and jongleurs sang. The epic *chansons de geste*, Songs of Deeds, about legendary heroes, were recited to lute accompaniments or sung in abbey and hostel halls along the road to Compostella and other pilgrim routes, and in the stone keeps that were rising all over Europe. Here the wandering jongleur was a welcome guest. As he sang of Charlemagne, Roland and Oliver in the most famous of the *gestes*, the *Song of Roland*, many of his listeners were preparing to join the First Crusade and had already fought against the infidel in Spain. They had seen the Moorish fleets in the Mediterranean which the jongleur described:

> *Huge are the forces of this detested race.*
> *The Paynims voyage, steering with oars and sail.*
> *On the tall prows and on the masts they raise*
> *Unnumbered lanterns and carbuncles ablaze;*
> *High overhead they throw out such a flame,*
> *The sea by night is beautiful and gay;*
> *And when they draw unto the land of Spain*
> *The whole coast shines and glitters in the rays.*

Taillefer, Duke William's minstrel, rode up and down before the Normans at the battle of Hastings singing the *Song*, rousing the fierce warriors to an even greater pitch of fervour. Indeed, the function of the jongleur at its highest during this heroic period when the steely Moslem ring was closing ever tighter round Christendom, was to rouse enthusiasm to fight the paynim everywhere, and especially to develop in the noble youths training in each castle, an ardour of courage and a resolve like Charlemagne's, 'Never to Paynims may I show love or peace'. For the theme of the song is the duty of Christian warriors to exterminate paganism. This was indeed the key theme of all Crusades, and to this end also the jongleurs devoted their talents, as they were, later, travelling to and fro in Europe, to write and sing ballads designed to promote the cause of freedom for the oppressed.

With the twelfth century, Europe was no longer on the defensive. A sentiment of pity and tenderness took the place of the warlike emotions of the eleventh. Art and literature and the songs and stories of the jongleurs reflected these changes. The period of chivalry began which lasted throughout the thirteenth century. Romance replaced epic and the 'gay science of love' from Provence toned down warrior emotions. The cult of the Virgin developed rapidly and the story of the jongleur is told who, after many wanderings and transgressions, found a home at last in the abbey of Clairvaux. Having no other offering for Our Lady he daily displayed in secret before her altar the tumbling tricks which had won him applause and money in the world.

The twelfth century is also the period of the *troubadours* of Provence, and the *trouvères* of northern France with their counterparts, the *minnesingers* of Germany. But these were often of royal and noble birth. Many were scholars and most were attached to courts. Some jongleurs were employed by them as assistants in the recitals they provided, and often enough the jongleurs on their travels sang songs they had learned from the troubadours. One of these songs written by Bernart de Ventadorn is still extant:

> *Since you ask me to sing, my lords, I will.*
> *Yet I weep when I try.*
> *My heart fills with tears.*
> *A sorrowful singer can sing but ill.*
> *Yet my passion is less than in former years.*
> *So why should I despair?*

Bernart's patron was the lovely Eleanor of Aquitaine who took him north with her when she became the wife of Henry II of England. Abelard has also been suggested as another writer and inspirer of troubadour songs, and we know that his were sung

46 Angel musicians playing trumpets, a harp, cittern, vielle and psaltery

with delight by jongleurs and ordinary folk throughout Christendom.

The thirteenth century was the age of happiness for the jongleurs and their German counterparts the *gauklei*. Merchants and the wealthy bourgeoisie provided new audiences. *Fabliaux*, which were lusty, humorous and gross, were recounted by the jongleurs, many of whom were gifted musicians and played the vielle, which was a type of violin played with a bow. This required great skill. Other instruments played by these wandering musicians are shown in a beautiful series of fourteenth-century sculptures at Exeter cathedral. These include the cittern, the bagpipe, the clarion, the rebec, the psaltery, the syrinx, the sackbut, the regals, the gittern, the shalm, the timbrel and the cymbals. Some of these can be seen, and recordings of their music heard, at the South Kensington Museum.

As the profession of jongleurs declined during the fourteenth century, fewer of their number could play the vielle. Instead they performed on naquaires, which were drums suspended from their waists, or on tambourines. The gleeman of the ballad *The king of England and the jongleur of Ely* played a tambourine.

> *He came thence to London and in a meadow there,*
> *Met with the king and all his meinie fair.*
> *Around his neck he carried his tabour,*
> *Enriched it was with gilt and bright azure.*

The decline of the jongleurs has been attributed to specialisation. In the past, minstrels had been extremely gifted and versatile. They could sing, act, play the buffoon, perform on several instruments with skill and even do a certain amount of juggling and tumbling, so that a small troupe could provide a full entertainment. But with the increase in sophistication and in education, more people were reading stories and poems for themselves. As the demand for wandering entertainers decreased, the standard of living and of the quality of their performances deteriorated. The public began to hold them in contempt as indeed the church had always done. Throughout the centuries the jongleurs 'of no settled habitation' were condemned officially.

> Then there are entertainers who do no work but commit criminal acts, who follow courts and utter lies and calumnies. Such wandering buffoons are condemned by the Apostolic See. It is forbidden to eat with them for they are idle, destructive and evil speakers.

So the thirteenth-century Thomas of Cobham describes them. Yet individual ecclesiastics gave them alms. In 1203–4 Bishop Wolfger of Passau entered into his account book: 'To an old *joculator* in a red tunic at Ferrara, ii sol.'

There had always been confreries or brotherhoods of jongleurs from the earliest times. One was centred at Fécamp in the eleventh century. But guilds and hospices were founded more frequently during the period of decline to provide security. In 1330 the jongleurs Jacques and Huet, who were popular and successful,

47 Wandering buffoons

founded a hospice in Paris to which the more prosperous performers could contribute. At first there was only one room and an old woman to care for the sick. But in 1331 they held a reunion of minstrels, each of whom contributed towards the hospice. They added a chapel and a priest and gained the pope's consent for a permanent chaplain, so that destitute, wandering jongleurs had a refuge in Paris when lack of work or sickness overtook them. Other hospices were founded in several countries around this period.

Jongleurs and minstrels employed by rulers and magnates were naturally more gifted and more prosperous than their vagabond brothers. They were always well paid and received many perquisites as well as salaries. John of Gaunt's minstrels in the fourteenth century held a yearly court at Tutbury, and in August the roads leading there were crowded with bands of travelling musicians who wished to vote at the election of the 'king' minstrel, and compete in the sports and musical competitions. Henry of Derby, Gaunt's son, probably chose his band of musicians at the Tutbury festival. They had 4d. a day during peace, but when on war service 6d. a day. They also had their gowns of russet rayed with blood and tan cloth. Gaunt granted his musicians a charter with certain privileges over other members of their profession, and the standard set at Tutbury promoted skill in good music in the five neighbouring counties.

Except for the higher paid and more gifted minstrels attached to kings' and magnates' households, the rest of the fraternity deteriorated until, by the end of the fifteenth century, they were mere dissolute performers in taverns.

Langland is very contemptuous of the jongleurs of the fourteenth century.

Ribalds, clowns, buffoons and ballad-mongers, these all get paid for their filth; but a man who always has Holy Scripture on his lips . . . is little enough loved. As for those who set themselves up as fools and jesters, making a living by false pretences, who make up tales and spew out their foul language and drink and dribble and make men gape at them—who ridicule others and slander those who refuse to tip them—these men know about as much about music and minstrelsy as Munde the Miller knows of the Latin language. If it were not for their dirty jokes no one would give them so much as a farthing for the New Year. Nowadays, entertainment and minstrelsy is nothing by lewdness, flattery and filthy stories.

48 Charles VI of France in a dance of wild men

As in most decadent periods, these later entertainers were always on the look out for something new. At the end of the fourteenth century mummers disguised as wild men or 'woodhouses'—probably from the natives of Ireland known by this term—performed as dancers. In 1393 Charles VI of France put on such an entertainment which ended in tragedy and almost in his own death. In the Hotel St Pol in Paris the king and his courtiers disguised themselves in flaxen dresses to resemble hair and entered a chamber chained together to dance before a court audience. The Duke of Orleans held a torch near one of the wild men to discover his identity. The flaxen robe burst into flames which spread quickly. The king was only saved by the promptitude of the young Duchess of Berri who flung her cloak over him. Another noble plunged into a tub of water. The other four perished.

Almost equally perilous to jongleurs were the political ballads which many of them sang as they went from place to place. Minstrels in Wales made their contribution to the cause of freedom by fomenting rebellion through singing patriotic songs. In 1402 Parliament passed an act against them. They composed songs in aid of popular movements such as the revolt in England in 1381. The refrain of

When Adam delved and Eve span
Who was then the gentleman,

sung widely by the peasants, became the text of John Ball's speech at Blackheath. While the ballads of Robin Hood, the upholder of the poor and oppressed, the opponent of all tyranny, were popular especially among the populace during the later Middle Ages.

There were of course many women entertainers among the lower ranks of jongleurs. These were mainly dancers who performed sword dances and acrobatics, balancing on the points of swords and aiding jugglers. They too went round with performing animals. But progressively, the profession of entertainer deteriorated until it became necessary to insist that those who had become the 'personification of all vices' should obtain a licence before becoming a jongleur, so that at least some official check could be kept upon them.

8

Wandering scholars

> There are two kinds of clerics; those who live in obedience to their head, the bishop; those who owe allegiance to no man, but follow their own will..... Free-lances and vagabonds, they embrace a life of baseness and wandering.

So wrote Isodore of Seville in the tenth century about the *gyrovagus* or wandering scholar. Yet, without wandering, especially in the period before the general development of cathedral schools and universities, no youth bent on higher education and advancement could have gained his training in letters. For, after the failure of Charlemagne's empire in the ninth century, the lamps he had lit, especially those of education, grew dim, though they continued to flicker in monastic and cathedral schools. These, however, were few and far between.

Ralph Glaber, himself for a time a *gyrovagus* and a one-time pupil of Abelard, declared that by the year 1000 there was hardly a 'personage', religious or secular, in Europe. Yet Glaber has exaggerated the dearth of scholars. The emergence of Gerbert alone, brilliant of intellect, voracious for learning, a gifted teacher and diplomatist, contradicts the historian's aspersion on the tenth century; and Gerbert, also was a *gyrovagus*; his ceaseless search for additional manuscripts, new knowledge, distinguished patrons and ever higher promotion, drove him from France to Spain, across to Italy, on to Germany, back to France and finally to the papal throne itself. He has fully earned the title of the most famous, though not the first, wandering scholar.

Gerbert started his meteoric career as an oblate in the monastic school of St Gerald of Aurillac where his genius soon outstripped the knowledge of his teachers in the subjects of the *trivium*— grammar, logic and rhetoric. The boy hungered for mathematical instruction. When, therefore, in 967, Borell II, Count of Barcelona, visited the monastery and, struck by Gerbert's brilliance, offered to take him to Spain, the youth was delighted. He had heard stories of the Moslem genius for mathematics and science, of their translation of Greek texts and of their diabolic dabbling in magic at Toledo. On that long journey into Spain the young Gerbert must have dreamed dreams of advancement, though none, perhaps of such splendour as reality proved.

Under Atto, Bishop of Vich, he studied mathematics and probably went on to the famous monastery of Ripoll, which specialised in music, chronology and arithmetic. Here, in the country between Barcelona and the Pyrenees, time had stood still and Gerbert was able to enjoy the privileges of Carolingian civilisation, which had been preserved through the policy of the counts of Catalonia—patrons of Ripoll and of the scholars who studied there. Besides being a personal friend as well as supporter of the ruling pope, Oliba, brother of the ruling count, and later abbot of Ripoll, was to become a correspondent of Gerbert.

Legend states that Gerbert studied for a time at Toledo. The powers in magic he gained there enabled him, it was rumoured, to construct a brazen head which solved all mathematical problems for him—a tale originating, perhaps, in the facility with which Gerbert manipulated the clumsy Roman numerals with the aid of the abacus, which he re-introduced to Europe. This was an ancient calculating board, and Gerbert gave much time to working out the processes of multiplication and division with the aid of this device.

From Spain, Gerbert, equipped with his new knowledge, went to Rome. Here he delighted the pope with his wit and brilliance. After meeting the Emperor Otto I there, he visited the imperial court and became imbued with Constantine's and Charlemagne's dream—to establish a Christian empire which would bring order to a chaotic world. First, however, Gerbert decided to go to Rheims to add the weapon of rhetoric to his already formidable armoury.

I have always studied to live well and to speak well, he wrote. For, although the former is more important than the latter, yet in public affairs, both are necessary. To be able to restrain with fair words the wills of lawless men is useful in the highest degree.

Gerbert found Rheims an intellectual paradise—abounding in

49 Teaching the use of a monochord

manuscripts, with five scriptoria regularly copying more, close at hand. Here, also, Gerbert developed his outstanding gifts as a teacher. Music, as well as mathematics and rhetoric occupied much of his time. He taught the use of the monochord as an instrument for gaining correctness of pitch, especially for organs which he insisted on using in musical studies. The fame of his teaching drew students across the roads of Europe even from far-distant Magdeburg.

He was ardent in his studies, and the number of his pupils increased from day to day. In Gaul itself, and throughout Germany, across the Alps and into Italy, even to the Adriatic, this great teacher's name was carried.

But fate was planning further journeys for him. While visiting Rome with the archbishop of Rheims, the now famous *scholasticus* —still in his mid-thirties—met Otto II at Pavia. Recognising in Gerbert the type of gifted cleric he was already using to govern the Italian church and nobles, the emperor created Gerbert Abbot of Bobbio in north-west Italy. Here he became involved in bitter struggles with surrounding magnates over their claims to church lands and, when Otto died in 983, Gerbert was forced to flee to the imperial palace at Pavia, where he was caught up in the intrigue and diplomacy over the succession to the Empire. Many years later Gerbert

50 The church of St Columban, Bobbio

became the tutor of the 16-year-old Otto III, who wrote: 'We humbly ask that the flame of your knowledge may fan our spirit until, with God's help, you kindle the lively genius of the Greeks to shine within us'. He became also, a member of the emperor's chapel devoting his gifts as a musician to its service. Then in 998 Gerbert left for Ravenna to become its archbishop for a single year only, since in 999 the papal throne became vacant, and Otto again wrote to Gerbert,

Beloved master, Father Gerbert, no one excels you in knowledge of the ancients or of the works of the church. No one understands our people, Germans, Franks, Italians, Spaniards, Poles as well as you. Your knowledge would strengthen both Church and Roman Empire, I suggest, therefore that you become Pope. Like the sun and moon which light the sky, we shall together direct the destinies of the whole round world.

It was the ancient dream of a theocratic empire revived. With pope and emperor closely allied, the glories of a christian Rome were to be restored. Just as Pope Sylvester I had aided Constantine, so Gerbert, taking the title of Sylvester II eagerly agreed to aid Otto.

Even when overwhelmed by the business of the papacy, however, Gerbert retained his interest in intellectual and mathematical pursuits and continued his voluminous correspondence. Writing to a cleric of Liège, Gerbert

greets his still beloved and ever to be cherished Adalbold with unchanging sincerity. . . . You have requested that if I have any geometrical figures you have not yet heard that I should send them to you. Owing to pressure of secular affairs I have been prevented from doing so earlier.

He then goes on to explain the difference between arithmetical and geometrical methods for finding the area of a triangle and encloses diagrams.

This pressure of secular business was the inevitable consequence of Gerbert's alliance with Otto. Had the young emperor lived as long as Charlemagne, there was a possibility that the dream they both envisaged might have become a reality. But Otto's untimely death caused even what had been accomplished to fade like some insubstantial pageant. Gerbert ended his restless life the following year, a life of constant journeying on four different levels. On the social plane he had travelled from peasant's cottage to the palace of the Pope; on the physical, he had journeyed in search of knowledge through the length and breadth of western Christendom; on the intellectual, he had proceeded from ignorance to heights unscaled since the fall of the Roman Empire. On the spiritual—who can judge in what direction he had travelled, or how far he had sacrificed principle to ambition? Strange legends were circulated that he had sold his soul for knowledge, and William of Malmesbury a near contemporary declared, 'So did he urge his fortunes, the devil aiding him', with a final word on Gerbert's sudden end while officiating at Mass in the Chapel of Jerusalem, 'His death was terrible'.

With the eleventh century the scholars are, many of them, writing poetry, especially in their youth. There is Baudri, Abbot of Bourgueil in the Loire valley which produced so many poets, and Marbod, *scholasticus* of Angers, and later Bishop of Rennes. A love of nature and the open country begins to revive, and with Marbod we leave Angers with its narrow streets and foul smells to journey to his uncle's farm. There, one spring day he sits and writes,

> *Growing grass and quiet woods with a west wind*
> *blowing,*
> *Light and gay. From the rocks a spring swift*
> *flowing.*
> *These with sweet country sounds have served*
> *to heal*
> *My mind, restored its peace which town and*
> *crowded streets did from it steal.*

There is Sigebert of Liège who, after a long journey, has slept sound. He wakens at dawn to hear the shrilling of the cock. Leaping from bed he flings back the wooden shutters to the warm spring sun, and soon is on the road, composing poetry to the rhythm of his stride.

> *With body rested and with mind refreshed*
> *To swing along. In flowering hedgerows wild*
> *The birds are singing. Even a weary man*
> *His tiredness would forget.*

But all *vagi* were not as carefree as Sigebert. Many clerics

lacking advancement, were disappointed, many more found their
lives tedious, their vows too strict. There is the unknown scholar
who had wandered from the Rhine valley and journeyed with his
song-book to St Augustine's monastery in Canterbury. He was
one who had failed to come to terms with the deprivations caused
by his vows. On his long journey he flung himself one morning
under some flowering hedge to eat his frugal lunch. He too was
a poet, and out came his tablet.

> *Softly blows the west wind,*
> *Warm the spring sun's rays,*
> *Here the earth before me,*
> *Her sweetness displays.*
>
> *Yet though fair spring rejoices,*
> *In leaf and flower and grain,*
> *My heart can feel no gladness,*
> *But only doubt and pain.*

Yet it was not only poet scholars who were swarming on the
roads of Christendom, bound for one of its famous schools at

51 Travelling scholars

52 Abelard teaching Helöise

Rheims, or Chartres, Tours or Orleans, for by the eleventh century serious students were leaving the longer established law schools in Bologna and Pavia, to sit under the famous teachers of the north—Fulbert, pupil of Gerbert, at Chartres, Anselm and Ralph at Laon and Odo of Tournai, of whom it was said:

Not only from France and Flanders and Normandy, but also from far distant Italy, Saxony and Burgundy, divers clerics flowed together in crowds to hear him daily; so that throngs of curious disputants filled the public squares of the city, and it appeared as if the citizens had abandoned other activities to devote themselves entirely to philosophy.

Gerbert himself had left Rome for the noted school at Rheims to learn logic. Lanfranc, later Archbishop of Canterbury, went from Pavia to Tours for its grammar and logic. Then in 1079 was born the 'most commanding intellectual figure of his age'— Abelard, who describes himself as a 'peripatetic', that is an itinerant scholar and student of Aristotle. Born in remote Brittany he surrendered his inheritance as the eldest son of a knight since

the more I learned, he writes, the more I became devoted to study. I journeyed through various provinces, disputing wherever the art of logic was flourishing. Finally, I reached Paris.

Abelard too was a poet and during the tragic and unsettled period which followed his marriage to Helöise he wrote both words and music for many songs, some, no doubt as he tramped the roads of France. Of these Helöise wrote:

But two gifts, lacking in other philosophers are specially yours for winning the heart of any woman—those of speaking and singing.

Your songs, some in the classic metre, some in the new, are set to such delightful melodies that they are unforgettable. Even the unlettered are singing them everywhere.

Several unsigned poems remain whose tragic beauty is such that they must surely have been written by Abelard for Helöise, after their separation.

> *Low in thy grave with thee*
> *Happy to lie,*
> *Since there's no greater thing, Love, left to do.*
> *And to live after thee*
> *Is but to die.*
> *For with but half a soul, what can Life do?*

> *Peace, oh my stricken lute!*
> *Thy strings are sleeping.*
> *Would that my heart could still*
> *Its bitter weeping.*

The twelfth century, when Abelard was teaching was the spring time of the intellectual life of western Christendom. It saw Peter the Venerable journeying to Spain, and Adelard of Bath to Syria and Cilicia in pursuit of Moslem manuscripts and learning. Greek manuscripts also were eagerly sought after. A medical student at Salerno heard that a copy of Ptolemy's *Almagest*, a work on astronomy, had arrived in Sicily. It had been brought from Constantinople by Aristippus, ambassador of Roger II of Sicily as a gift from the emperor. To the brilliant court of Palermo, lodestone for scholars Greek, Latin, Moslem and Jewish, the Salernian student struggled: 'braving the terrors of Scylla and Charybdis, and the fiery streams of Etna, he found Aristippus at Pergusa, near the fountain, engaged, not without danger, in investigating the marvels of Etna.' But although the student knew some Greek, it was not enough to translate the technicalities of the *Almagest* into Latin. He was fortunate, however, in finding Eugene, 'fluent in Greek, Arabic and Latin', and with his help, after two years of effort, the manuscript was made available for western scholars 'who had no Greek'. It was not the Salernian version, however, which became the standard text for the universities, but one made in 1175 by a later and more famous translator, Gerard of Cremona.

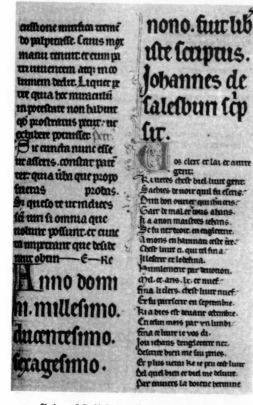

John of Salisbury—one of Abelard's pupils—was another of the wandering scholars of the early twelfth century. He went when 'but a lad' to Paris, practically penniless and often, but for the kindness of friends, on the verge of starvation. After attending the school at Chartres where he received a thorough grounding in grammar, he returned to Paris, then secured a secretaryship with Theobald and the succeeding Archbishops of Canterbury, Thomas Becket and Richard. On their behalf he made many journeys, some to the court of the English pope, Hadrian IV, whose personal friend he was.

53 John of Salisbury's holograph lesson book

I have ten times passed the chain of the Alps, John wrote, on my road from England. I have twice traversed Apulia. The business of my lords and friends I have often transacted in the Roman church and for various causes have many times travelled not only round England, but round Gaul.

John naturally spent a great deal of his time writing letters which became popular reading until the sixteenth century. He was the best read scholar of his time, had travelled extensively, met some of the most famous people of his age and, by the vividness of his style can bring them before us and also recreate the very atmosphere of the places he visited. We shudder in the Alps with him as he writes:

Pardon me for not writing. I have been on the mount of Jove; on one side gazing up to the heaven of the mountains, on the other, appalled by the hell of the valleys. . . . 'Lord,' I prayed, 'restore me to my brethren, that I may warn them not to visit this place of torment.' . . . I put my hand in my scrip so as to write a word or two. Lo, I found my ink but a block of ice; my fingers refused to write, my beard was frozen, my very breath turned to a long icicle—I was quite unable to write as I wished.

On another occasion during his travels, John describes a feast given by Pope Hadrian in Apulia where 'delicacies from Constantinople, Alexandria, Tripoli and Tyre' were provided.

John also supported Becket in his struggle against King Henry believing that the authority of the spiritual should control the secular power. He shared Becket's exile and was his 'truest because his wisest friend'.

It was to obtain positions similar to that of John, at the court of kings, archbishops and princes, that students of the twelfth and thirteenth century swarmed across the roads of Christendom, willing to travel, suffer hardship and hunger, for the sake of the scholarship necessary to advancement. Bologna and Pavia were the goals of those who sought a training in law while Paris excelled in theology. So many foreign students came to these centres that they divided into 'nations', each of which was

54 A doctor of law and students

organised into a guild or *universitas*. On several occasions these guilds left Bologna *en masse*, migrating to Padua in protest against town statutes which discriminated against them. With the Pope's support, they gained the right to elect their own rectors and to have laws and regulations of their own. In Bologna at the beginning of the thirteenth century the nations were divided into Ultramontane and Cismontane. The former group consisted of fourteen separate nations—the French, Spanish, Provençal, English, Picard, Burgundian, Poitvin, Touranian, Norman, Catalonian, Hungarian, Polish, German and Gascon—which gives some idea of the vast numbers of scholars on the move from time to time throughout Europe. A twelfth-century monk writes:

> These wandering clerks are wont to roam about the world and visit all its cities till much learning makes them mad; for in Paris they seek the liberal arts, in Orleans classics, at Salerno medicine, at Toledo magic, but nowhere manners or morals.

Perhaps it was possible when meeting such students on the road to distinguish to which nation each belonged, if the twelfth-century dictum of Jacques de Vitry is true, for he states:

> The English are drunkards and have tails; the sons of France are carefully adorned like women; Germans are obscene at their feasts; Normans boastful; Poitvins traitors and always adventurers.

The remaining nations receive equally insulting descriptions.

55 A doctor of law lecturing. (From the tomb of Lorenzo Pini, Jun.)

With the development of Paris as an intellectual centre streams of students from every part resorted there. 'The men of intellect have emigrated to Gaul', one historian declared. Dissillusionment often followed. As the numbers of scholars increased, many of them found that advancement did not come their way. Some then joined the ranks of *goliards*—light of heart, disreputable, and penniless—they roamed the roads, putting up at monasteries, begging or joining the ranks of the jongleurs, if they had gifts as musicians, storytellers or singers. Others pawned their remaining books, or merely lost them, many more paid them over at dice as one of them describes:

56 An imperial banquet. Out-of-work scholars became mummers and entertainers at times

> *Each man asks and each will spier*
> *What has come of all my gear?*
>
> *Dice hath cost me all my gear.*
> *Turned my revel into woe,*
> *Never a town in France I know*
> *Where I've not left some book behind.*
> *At Gandalus above La Ferté,*
> *There I left my A.B.C.*
> *My 'Paternoster' at Soissons,*
> *And my 'Credo' at Monléon,*
> *My 'Seven Psalms' are at Tournai*
> *My 'Fifteen Psalms' are at Cambrai.*
>
> *Back I came through Pontarlie*
> *And there I sold my 'Litany'*
> *And at the town of the great salt mine,*
> *I drank my Missal down in wine.*

So he gaily continues, leaving his Antiphonary, his Donatus and Ovid, his Tobit and his Doctrinale, innumerable tattered clues of his irresponsible journey through France. Thus, having lost his few possessions, the student was forced to beg, like a certain Burnellus in the twelfth century on his way to the schools in Paris who, 'being poor and his purse light, stopped often on the road to beg'. Or perhaps like another student vagabond, he put his prayer into verse, addressing the magnate who had given him shelter for the night—

> *I, a wandering scholar lad,*
> *Born for toil and sadness,*
> *Oftentimes am driven by*
> *Poverty to madness.*
>
> *Literature and knowledge I*
> *Fain would still be earning,*
> *Were it not that want of pelf*
> *Makes me cease from learning.*
>
> *O thou pride of N————,*
> *By thy worth I pray thee*
> *Give the suppliant help in need,*
> *Heaven will sure repay thee.*

Begging, in fact, became so common among students that it was enacted that no scholar should ask alms on the highways until the Chancellor of his university, having satisfied himself on the merits of each individual case, granted a certificate to the applicant.

Other students who wished to make a good impression at home acquired a set of books bound in calf skin and walked, bent double under their weight, hoping their parents, impressed by the splendour of these manuscripts, would take it for granted that they had passed their examinations.

But most goliards—the true vagabond scholars—were careless of the opinion of parents or society. They shot their bolts of ridicule wherever they found ecclesiastical abuses, not sparing the pope himself. Above all, they flaunted the joys of youth in frankly sensual and pagan verse, often of the highest literary merit, and sang the praises of wine, women and song, not forgetting the dice box. But above all else, they valued poetry; it was probably the Archpoet who wrote:

> Should a tyrant rise and say,
> 'Give up wine!' I'd do it;
> 'Love no girls!' I would obey,
> Though my heart should rue it.
> 'Dash thy lyre!' suppose he saith,
> Naught should bring me to it;
> 'Yield thy lyre or die!' my breath,
> Dying, should thrill through it!

If only for their contribution to medieval Latin poetry, while not forgetting their unquenchable gaiety of spirit under poverty and the harshest suffering, the goliards should be remembered. Indeed, their *Gaudeamus Igitur* has defied time's extinction through the centuries, remaining a widely popular student song until modern times. Sung, at least until recently by German students after the funeral of a comrade, it proclaims the joys of youth, defying care even while the evidence of death is before them.

> Let us live then, and be glad
> While young life's before us!
>   After youthful pastime had,
>   After old age hard and sad,
> Earth will slumber o'er us.
>
> Perish cares that peak and pine!
> Perish envious blamers!
>   Die the Devil, thine and mine!
>   Die the starch-necked Philistine!
> Scoffers and defamers!

9

Doctors and the diseased

During the entire Middle Ages and beyond, supernatural aid was regarded as one of the most powerful means of healing sickness and bodily infirmities. Divine power was thought to operate most effectively where the body or relics of a saint or martyr were preserved. Consequently Christians undertook arduous and often dangerous journeys to visit these shrines.

St Bernard of Clairvaux in the twelfth century vigorously supported this belief asserting:

> to buy drugs, to consult physicians, to take médicines befits not religion and is contrary to purity. He taught like St James, 'Is any sick among you? Let him call for the elders of the Church and let them pray over him . . . and the prayer of faith shall heal the sick.'

Following out this teaching a young paralytic of the eleventh century placed entire confidence in the power of prayer and the saints to cure his affliction. He visited shrines in France, Germany, Ireland, Belgium and Italy, ending at the tomb of St James of Compostella yet without success. At last, however, at Conques in France, the use of his limbs was restored at the shrine of Ste Foy.

Later, with the development of the Cult of the Virgin, prayer and offerings at her shrine were regarded as especially efficacious. During the fifteenth century Margaret Paston wrote to her husband in London:

> Thank God for your amending of the great disease that you have had. . . . My mother behested another image of wax of the weight of you to Our Lady of Walsingham and she sent four nobles to the four orders of friars in Norwich to pray for you. I have behested to go on pilgrimage to Walsingham and St Leonard's for you.

These examples show that it was not expected that cures by

faith would occur instantaneously, nor without expenditure of effort and money on the part of the sufferer, or on his behalf. There was also a converse side to this belief in the power of God and his saints, for among the illiterate peasantry of Europe paganism persisted, disguised under the merest veneer of Christianity. The ancient customs and spells, even the ancient gods were still regarded as potent, and the sick were carried, often long distances, to groves regarded as sacred, though condemned by the Church as evil. Regarding these beliefs the eleventh-century chronicler Glaber states: 'Men must beware of the manifold errors of demons, or of men, which abound everywhere in the world. More especially in the matter of springs and groves incautiously venerated by sick folk.' In the thirteenth century, superstition was still as rife. The brilliant preacher, Bernold of Regensburg, says, 'Many of the village folk would come to heaven it not for their witchcrafts'. Fra Bernadino (1380–1444) also constantly warns his hearers in Italy against witchcraft and sorcery.

Does a child seem ailing? The mother's first thought is that it has been bewitched. Off she hastens to the lonely cottage of the local witch to buy a more powerful charm, inscribed with words which cannot be understood. This she hangs round the child's neck on the hair from a virgin's head and so hopes to draw down power against the original spell. But it is the Devil who will draw down both mother and child to the accursed house.

57 A doctor of Physic

Yet Christian charms were not condemned by the Church and even established physicians used them. In the library at York Minster the medicine book of William Leech de Killingholme has been preserved. It is dated 1412 and the servant of the physician probably carried this book in his

master's bag of instruments as they rode across the flat Lincolnshire roads to visit patients. Included in it is a charm against
fevers which probably proved useful on occasions to a country
leech.

> I adjure you, ye fevers, by the Father, the Son and the Holy Ghost,
> by Emmanuel, Sabaoth, Adonai and the Mediator, by prophet and
> priest, by the signs of the Zodiac . . . by Jesus Christ and in virtue of
> His blood, . . . and because you have no power to hurt. . . . In the
> Name of the Father, the Son and the Holy Ghost.

Herbal remedies also were widely used. William was sure to
own a herbarium containing beautifully drawn illustrations of
herbs and plants, with recipes for their use and directions as to
the diseases which they helped to cure, for most physicians
believed 'there is no herb or weed but God has given virtue to
them, to help man'. Indeed, it was very likely that William would
ride firmly clutching a bunch of mugwort since his herbarium
stated: 'If any propose to make a journey, let him take in hand
mugwort. Then he will not feel much toil from travelling.' If still
young and inexperienced as a physician, William's servant might
hear him muttering the various herbal cures he must remember.
Yarrow for toothache and hardness of the veins; rue for nose
bleeding and weakness of the eyes; groundsel for gout and dock
for swollen glands—the number of useful herbs was endless. So
unhappily, were the ills they were thought to cure.

Physicians and leeches were not alone in their use of herbs
as medicines. The *triacleurs*, who administered treacle as one of
their cures, were quacks who visited fairs and markets, selling
pills, salves and potions, for which they claimed the most miracu-
lous results. They often teamed up with pardoners who, like
themselves, depended on their wit and the slickness of their
tongues to bring in groats and pennies from their credulous
hearers. Their style of patter changed little from the earliest
centuries to modern times. After banging his drum or blowing his
trumpet at the fair a quack might begin:

> The Sultan Gilgal being violently afflicted with a spasmus came six
> hundred leagues to meet me in a go-cart. I gave him so speedy an
> acquitance of his dolor that next night he danced a saraband with
> flip-flaps (cartwheels) and somersets.

58 Triacleur (with drum) and false pardoners

Awestruck yet entertained, the simple peasants would be eager
to buy the remedy which had worked so potently on a Sultan.
Yet the triacleur was far from being as gullible himself. In an
amusing medieval farce a quarrel between a pardoner and one
of these quacks breaks out at an inn. The pardoner is proudly
displaying his relics—the snout of St Antony's pig, a seraph's
feather stamped by God. But here the triacleur rudely interrupts.
'Blood of God!' he shouts, 'Tis but the quill of the very goose he
ate for dinner.'

Certain medieval diseases, or rather legislation concerning
them, actually forced many sufferers on to the open road. Leprosy
was one of these, and those infected by it often became outcasts
from society. They were forbidden to enter inns, mills or bake-
houses, to touch healthy persons or to eat with them, to wash in
streams or walk on narrow foot-paths. Even in churches, special
places apart were assigned to them and a separate holy-water
stoup. Laws were made from time to time barring them from
entering towns at all. In 1346 lepers were forbidden to enter
London and in 1375 the porters of its gates were sworn to prevent
them from entering or staying in the city or its suburbs. A law in
France evicted them from Paris in 1488.

59 Leper begging

Leper houses were built for these sufferers, but not until the disease had become a menace to public health. These hospices were placed outside towns. Lanfranc, Archbishop of Canterbury, built one in the woods of Blean, a mile from the west gate, in 1084. A sketch of the leper hospital of St Giles-in-the-Fields was drawn by Mathew Paris in 1222 in the margin of his manuscript. It was well in the country and shows a tower over the east end, a smaller one on the west porch, a chapel and a hall. It housed 40 lepers. Numerous as these lazarettos were, especially during the twelfth century, there must have been many sufferers who by temperament or from lack of accommodation wandered the roads, begging. The dolorous clanging of the bell or the ominous sound of the clacker they carried, warned travellers of their approach, and these hastily made a detour to avoid the shrouded forms, fearing contagion.

Fevers with rashes, syphilis and other diseases were often confused with leprosy, and those who suffered from them were also expelled at times from the towns. But the epidemic which caused the greatest disturbance to the greatest number in medieval Europe was undoubtedly the Black Death. It entered western Christendom as the result of one of the most ill-fated voyages in the story of travel. Gabriel de Mussis, a jurist of Piacenza, Italy, was a passenger on one of the ships which brought the plague to Europe and has left an eye-witness account of what happened. He had been practising among the Genoese and Venetian merchants who had settled in Tana on the Don and in Caffa, on the Crimean Straits of Kertch. These merchants had been besieged for three years by Tartar hordes in Caffa. Gabriel relates:

The merchants and others, crowded within the walls, could scarcely breathe. They were partially relieved by the arrival of a ship bearing supplies. Then plague broke out among the Tartars who flung their dead inside the walls by means of siege engines so that infection spread to the dwellers in the fort.

Unexpectedly the Tartars fled and those who had survived the siege and plague set sail in four ships, calling first at Constantinople. Later, in the Aegean, this fateful flotilla separated.

Thus it happened that our fleet, manned by sailors infected with poisonous disease arrived at Genoa, some at Venice and some in other Christian regions. Because of the grievous affection that was upon us, of a thousand making the voyage, scarcely ten survived.

On reaching land, those who remained carried 'shafts of death' to their relatives and friends and the plague spread swiftly through Europe. Later, a merchant vessel carrying infected woollen goods from London arrived in Bergen full of corpses, and so took the Black Death to Norway.

All kinds of precautions were taken to try to stop the spread of the disease, but proved useless. Many took to flight, hoping to escape. So great was the exodus from England that in 1349, a proclamation gave out:

Forasmuch as no mean part of our people of England is dead in the

60 Burial of plague victims

present pestilence . . . and numbers are daily passing, or proposing to pass, to parts overseas with money which they were able to have kept within the realm . . . we do command the mayor and bailiffs of Sandwich (and 48 other ports) to stop the passage beyond sea of those without a mandate.

Nevertheless during the sporadic outbreaks of plague in Europe during the following centuries, flight became increasingly one of the commonest means adopted to escape from this dread disease. In 1383 many fled in terror when plague broke out in Florence, and Niccolo, brother-in-law of the merchant Francesco Datini of Prato, wrote to him: 'The plague waxes in various places and spreads in this direction. . . . People are much afraid and the deaths are beginning. . . . In God's name we will send you our boy Pippo.' In an effort to stop the exodus from the city the Senate decreed that none should leave; but in vain, and Niccolo decided to flee with his family, but wrote again: 'My boy Nanni was stricken and in a day and a half we buried him. In Florence the destruction fills one with pity.'

During the Middle Ages it was believed that disease was one form of punishment for sin. Consequently, throughout the fourteenth century, but especially during periods of plague, the roads of Europe witnessed long processions of penitents who went from place to place, scourging themselves as penance for their transgressions, praying at shrines, singing psalms and hymns and

61 Procession of Flagellants

proclaiming the coming of 'a holy Communism' like that which the early Christians had enjoyed. These flagellants were mainly craftsmen and peasants, poor and illiterate. Their demonstrations were condemned both by wealthy merchants and by many in authority, both lay and ecclesiastical. But they were hailed with joy by the unfortunate and discontented.

In August 1399 the ravages of plague in Italy had become so terrible that even hard-headed traders like Francesco Datini and leading ecclesiastics like the Bishop of Fiesole near Florence 'resolved to go on pilgrimage, clothed entirely in white linen and barefoot. . . . For at that time a great number of Christians throughout the world made the same resolve.' Thirty thousand went in Datini's company carrying lighted candles out of Florence 'scourging themselves with a rod, accusing themselves of sin', having sworn to eat no meat, nor take off their clothes nor sleep in a bed for the nine days that they trudged to Arezzo and back. Nevertheless Francesco writes: 'I took with me two horses and a mule which carried two saddle chests containing boxes of comfits, many cheeses, fresh bread and biscuits, round cakes and other things needful to a man's life. . . . I also took a great sack of warm raiment.' For although Francesco constantly paid lip service and gave generously to the poor and the church, like the majority of medieval Christians he was not deeply spiritual. He therefore performed his pilgrimage in comparative comfort and on his return—obviously doubting the efficacy of his penance and prayers—booked a house in Bologna and with his wife, his men-servants and maid-servants, his laden mules and asses, fled incontinently from the dreadful pestilence.

Certain nervous disorders also drove vast numbers on to the roads. In some cases these were children, and the symptoms of hysteria and excitement displayed appear similar to some outbreaks at modern sessions of crooners and singers. In 1212 a shepherd boy, Etienne in Vendome, gave out that the Lord Himself had appeared to him and given him a letter to the King. Neighbouring shepherd boys joined him and were thrown into ecstasies by the power of his words. On reaching St Denis followed by an army of children he performed miracles and began to preach a children's crusade. Innumerable other children joined and in July this vast army set out for Marseilles, carrying oriflammes, wax candles, crosses and censers. They sang hymns with fervid emotion and believed that when they reached the sea,

62 The dancing mania

it would roll back at Etienne's command and let them reach Jerusalem dry-shod. A similar incident occurred at the same time in Germany under a boy named Nicolas. Twenty-five years later in Erfurt a wave of religious excitement among its children impelled them to go leaping and dancing by the Steigerwald to Armstadt. The two original crusades ended tragically. Many children died en route, many became victims of evil people who took possession of them, but the majority were enticed on to ships at Marseilles, taken to Alexandria and Bougia and sold as slaves to the Saracens.

These outbreaks had a resemblance to the strange illness known in medieval times as the 'dancing mania' or tarantism, since it was by some supposed to result from the bite of the tarantula spider. It was also called the dance of St John or St Vitus, from the gigantic leaps performed by those afflicted by the mania. It appeared first in 1374 at Aix-la-Chapelle when a procession of men and women arrived from Germany, made their way to the square, and after joining hands danced round in circles, working themselves into a frenzy, foaming at the mouth, and contorting their bodies until they fell down at last, exhausted. Processions of dancers went from town to town, being joined en route by peasants from the fields, mechanics from their workshops and women from their homes, while gangs of vagabonds took advantage of the disturbances to increase the confusion, and rob and pillage empty houses and shops.

This mental contagion spread through the Netherlands, into Germany and south into Italy. Its true origin is to be sought in the unbearable conditions left by the Black Death, by disastrous floods in Germany, followed by famine and misery, and by the incessant feuds of magnates in Europe. The oppression of the populace in most countries resulting in moral degradation also helped to cause an upsurge of insoluble mental conflict. The only relief for many was the intoxication of mental delirium which took the form of wild and uncontrolled dancing. Boccaccio wrote regarding the disease, 'Neither the advice of any physician, nor the virtue of any medicine prevailed.' Unfortunately this was the case with regard to much illness in the Middle Ages, since doctors were seldom able to diagnose the causes of disease correctly. Moreover thousands of sufferers were left to wander homeless, penniless and untended along the roads of medieval Christendom. Among these were also found the mentally deranged, who called out Langland's pity:

> Lunatic vagrants who are more or less mad according to the phases of the moon. These care neither for cold nor heat, wandering after money over many wide counties, without understanding, but with no evil intent.

Nevertheless, monasteries and abbeys, as well as leprosaries and hospitals specially built by pious individuals like that which still exists at Beaune in France, testify to considerable concern during the Middle Ages that the helpless and ailing poor should find care and shelter if they chose to seek it.

10

Masons, sculptors and carpenters

When the poet Lydgate about 1415 describes how Priam set
about building Troy he tells us that the king

> *Made seek in every region*
> *For such workmen as were curious,*
> *Of wit inventive, of casting marvellous,*
> *Of such as knew the craft of geometry*
> *Or were subtle in their fantasy;*
> *And for every such that was good deviser*
> *Mason, hewer or crafty quarryer,*
> *For every craftsman and passing carpenter*
> *That may be found either far or near.*
>
> *He sent also for every imager*
> *That could draw or with colour paint*
> *With hues fresh that the work not faint.*
>
> *Thus Priam for every master sent*
> *For each carver and gifted joiner*
> *To make knots with many curious flower.*

This scene is set against the medieval background which the
poet knew, not in the far distant age of the Trojan War. Lydgate
was well aware that the chief problem in erecting a medieval
building was to attract skilled workmen to sites which were often
remote. By the thirteenth and fourteenth century men were re-
cruited not only from distant parts of their own country, but they
were brought in from foreign lands to work. Indeed as early as
the eighth century a chronicler tells us: 'How many buildings
Wilfrid (bishop of Ripon and of York) brought to perfection. . . .
Many by the advice of masons whom the hope of liberal reward
had drawn thither from Rome.'

In the late fourteenth century, English or Irish masons were working on the abbey of Batalha in Portugal, and in 1387 master masons from all over Europe were invited to give advice on plans projected for a cathedral at Milan. Indeed throughout the Middle Ages craftsmen connected with the building trade, whether master masons, mere hewers and quarriers, artists, sculptors, carpenters or smiths, were mostly itinerant. In fact it was often necessary to impress men to serve, for only cathedrals and colleges were allowed to retain a permanent body of builders, so that building craftsmen were often itinerant by com-

63 *The self-sculptured figure of Adam Kraft of Nuremburg, master mason, (c. 1455–1508) placed under his masterpiece, the Tabernacle in the church of St Lorenz*

pulsion. These workers were trained at some great quarry or in a lodge attached to some important building that was being erected. At these lodges, especially if distant from a town, huts called 'mansiones' were built, where the men could eat and sleep. Usually a larger hut or 'loge' served for a workshop and tool shop. Strict rules were drawn up for the workers, and a master mason was elected to preside over the lodge.

Since the earlier freemasons were necessarily journeymen who travelled widely to their employment, the usual system of apprenticeship which prevailed in most other trades was impossible, at least before the evolution of shop sculptors in the fourteenth century. Tools and material were supplied by employers who did not wish either to be spoilt by unskilled workers. The only apprentices, therefore, were those of the master mason, and the employers was protected by strict rules from bad work which might be done by them. In 1480, for instance, it was decreed:

That if it befall that any mason that be perfect and cunning come for to seek work and find any unperfect working, the master of the place shall receive the perfect and do away with the unperfect, to the profit of his lord.

This dispersion of many skilled craftsmen throughout Christendom resulted in a wide dissemination of ideas and of styles of building. Closer contact with the east through the Norman conquest of southern Italy and Sicily in the eleventh century, and the conquest of Barbastro in north-east Spain by French and Normans, also had the same effect. Among the thousands of Moorish prisoners taken were singers, musicians and a corps of engineers, skilled in the erection of fortresses and defence works. Seven thousand of these Moslems from Barbastro were sent to Constantinople, 1500 to Rome and several thousand to France. As a result a new stream of culture, knowledge and techniques flowed into that of western Europe and Byzantium.

Frankish engineers returning from their successes in the First Crusade had brought back first-hand knowledge of Byzantine, Armenian and Saracen castles and defences. Prisoners, skilled in planning and construction also brought new ideas into the west. One of these, called Lalys, built Neath Abbey in Glamorganshire. What is probably the first European ribbed vault—that in Durham cathedral—is thought to be eastern in origin, as is the pointed arch.

Artists, friars and explorers like Marco Polo, who penetrated into China and the Far East, brought back not only ideas but sometimes drawings and detailed notes of what they had seen, including some of buildings. Under Edward I an English embassy of which Robert the sculptor was a member was sent to Persia, so that it is significant that, during the closing years of the thirteenth century, patterns resembling Persian diaper work appear on English buildings. Two Franciscans, one an artist, went to Cairo and Palestine in 1323. On the tomb of Mustapha Pasha in Cairo (1269–73) decorations in the form of straight hexagons within a Gothic arch are used, instead of curvilinear tracery as in the west. From this use of straight lines instead of curves, it is thought that the English perpendicular style was developed.

An Austin friar, Frate Giovanni, recorded plans and drawings of buildings seen on his travels in Europe and Asia. One of a roof in a palace 'in India beyond the sea' became his model for the great timber roof at Padua in the Ragione palace which he designed in 1306.

Master masons also were travelling from all parts of Europe during the fourteenth and fifteenth centuries to attend guild conferences. The Master of the Strasbourg Lodge had jurisdiction over the masons of the Empire with subordinate lodges at Berne, Cologne and Vienna. Some master masons travelled as far as five hundred miles to attend congresses, bringing their problems and new ideas to discuss with their fellow architects. They also travelled widely to act as consultants, or to plan and superintend the erection of cathedrals and other buildings. Enrique de Burgos (d. 1277) who built Burgos and Leon cathedrals in Spain was probably a Frenchman. William of Sens, named from his birthplace designed the new choir of Canterbury cathedral (1175–78). Etienne de Bonneil left Paris in 1287 to act as master mason for the building of the cathedral at Upsala, Sweden.

During his journeyman days an aspiring master mason would spend much time learning geometrical and numerical formulae and how to set out a building from examples drawn by his master on the cathedral floor where he was working. Designs for major buildings were made on parchment skins. Examples can still be seen in Strasbourg and Vienna. One of these master masons, the twelfth-century Villard de Honnecourt, has left a sketch book from which it is possible to deduce a good deal concerning his everyday life. He was a great traveller, visiting Rheims, Chartres, Meaux and many other places. While in Rheims he received a summons to work in Hungary where King Bela was rebuilding towns destroyed by invading Tartars. There is evidence that Villard was the architect who reconstructed part of Cambrai cathedral and that Elizabeth of Hungary, King Bela's sister, because of her devotion to Our Lady of Cambrai, contributed funds towards the rebuilding of the transepts. Elizabeth may have been instrumental in Villard's being summoned from France to work in far distant Hungary. On the sketch of a window which he made when in Rheims he has written: 'This is a window at Rheims. . . . I had been summoned to Hungary when I drew it, so I like it all the more.' Above he has outlined a beautiful Madonna and Child, perhaps as a remembrance of Our Lady of Cambrai connected in his mind with Elizabeth of Hungary.

Villard also on his visit to Laon drew the tower of the church with its stone oxen peering from open porticos placed diagonally across the angles. The design delighted him, and he writes, 'I have visited many countries as this book shows. But never have I seen a tower to equal this of Laon.' There are many lifelike impressions of animals and insects recorded as Villard journeyed through woodland and mountain to Austria—a crouching hare, a boar in flight, a stag, as well as studies of a dragon fly, a grass-hopper, a horse-fly and a snail. His crouching cat is not so realistic, having a smirk reminiscent of Alice's Cheshire cat in Wonderland. Villard must have visited a nobleman's zoo on one of his journeys for he has drawn a lion with his tamer, accompanied by two small dogs. Of this sketch he writes:

64 The tower of Laon, France

I wish to tell you about the training of a lion. His trainer has two small dogs. He gives an order to the lion who may growl instead of obeying. Then the tamer beats the dogs. The lion is so perplexed at this that he does as he is bid. But if he is thoroughly enraged, then he is unmanageable for good and ill. And remember, this lion was drawn from life.

An amusement gallery was sometimes run in conjunction with a medieval zoo. One existed at the castle of Hesdin (Artois). In these galleries visitors—who doubtless enjoyed the horseplay involved —were soaked to the skin on pulling the handle of one of the machines, then found themselves precipitated through a trap-door into a sack filled with feathers or even soot, when they tried to run away. Villard apparently felt impelled to invent some of his own mechanical absur-

65 Villard de Honnecourt's sketch of a lion and tamer

dities after visiting one of these galleries, for he has drawn an eagle, showing strings and pulleys arranged in its hollow body, and has labelled this: 'How to make the eagle turn his head to the deacon during the reading of the Gospel.' Another sketch is of the so-called Tantalus cup which shows a bird on a tower within a drinking bowl. The tower concealed a tube which acted as a syphon. When wine poured into the vessel had reached a certain level, the liquid disappeared. If the inner tube was not plugged at its foot, the would-be drinker was deluged with wine, which no doubt added to the merriment of the onlookers.

To go through Villard's album is to obtain glimpses of scenes, people and places he actually saw on his travels. There is a musician playing a viol while one of his dogs dances. The other animal however, maddened by the sight of a parrot held on the wrist of a woman in the audience, springs up towards the bird. Another time Villard records his visit to a Gallo-Roman tomb writing under it: 'This is the representation of a Saracen's tomb I saw once.' To medieval Christians of the Crusading era, all pagans, including the ancient Romans, were Saracens.

On his way to Hungary Villard admired a rose window in a church at Lausanne but must have drawn it from memory as the design differs radically from the actual window. A more interesting record of his passage through Switzerland is his study of two wrestlers, obviously drawn from life. This was a favourite sport of the Swiss and matches were regularly organised. One of these, Villard with his insatiable interest in subjects which might be utilised in his work, must have attended. In the church of

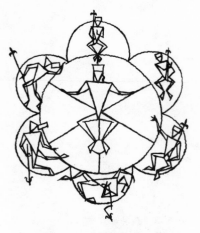

*66 Villard de Honnecourt's design
for a Wheel of Fortune*

Lausanne another artist has carved two wrestlers on a bas-relief in one of the stalls. Possibly Villard merely copied this, but his own drawing has every indication that it is the record of an actual scene.

Another interesting sketch in the album is that of a Wheel of Fortune which Villard has designed for a rose window with six foils. Fortune is seated in the centre, her feet on a globe. She holds a spoke in each hand and so turns it. A crowned and sceptred king sits at the top of the wheel. On his left, kings are shown falling from power. On his right, the wheel is returning them to affluence. All the figures are portrayed according to Villard's 'geometric method' of drawing to which he devotes a section in the album. Possibly he may have seen the wheel sculptured round the rose window at the north front of the church of St Etienne at Beauvais. Or perhaps, on his travels he stopped to watch a mechanical Wheel of Fortune. These were often placed inside churches to warn Christians to distrust the fickle goddess who bestowed favours only as capriciously to take them away. The Bishop of Dole refers to one of these moving wheels in the Abbey church of Fécamp, at the end of the eleventh century.

The last two entries in the album bring Villard before us in a very human way. He addresses those for whom he has written the book directly: 'Remember what I tell you. This potion will cure any wound that you may have.' He carefully directs that certain herbs shall be infused in white wine, adding 'Do not drink too much at a time, an eggshell will contain enough for a dose'. Accidents must have been frequent on medieval building sites and Villard is anxious to share knowledge which had perhaps proved efficacious in his own case.

Through his final entry we see him early on the road, gathering wild flowers, which he can allocate to their species.

Gather flowers of different colours in the morning. Do not let them touch each other. Take a sort of stone which can be cut with a chisel, and see that it be white and reduced to a fine powder. Lay your flowers in this, each according to their species. In this way you will preserve the colour of the flowers.

Although the sketches were mostly made during Villard's working life, the comments were added later, perhaps when he was old and about to hand over his album to a favourite apprentice or group of young craftsmen. Many wills are extant in which master masons leave money or goods to their apprentices. To those who were to receive his book he writes: 'Villard de Honnecourt salutes you and implores all who labour at the different kinds of work found in this book to pray for his soul and to hold him in re-membrance.'

Another twelfth-century artist, Gislebertus the sculptor of Autun, has left indications in his actual work of his interests and way of life. We know that he also travelled at least from Cluny to Autun, on to Vézelay and back to Autun. He was an accomplished artist when he arrived at Cluny but we have no indication of his wanderings during his journeyman days. Gislebertus, like many outstanding figures of medieval, or indeed of any times, travelled ahead of his contemporaries on the aesthetic plane, and this fact appears in his work. In the first place he escaped from the anony-mity which shrouded the work of many medieval artists, for above the west door of the cathedral of Autun, an inscription *Gislebertus hoc fecit* in the centre of the Last Judgement scene of the tympanum, attracts the eye. It is immediately below the sculp-tured Christ, and stands out not so much in homage but in pride. Much can be learned about the artist from this signature alone. In the first place, Gislebertus must have gained the consent of the bishop and chapter to have carved his name so prominently. The inference is that they also were proud to have it there. Already Gislebertus was a sculptor of note. Also of experience, for he had carved practically all the capitals that were prominent in the church. Only two which can be seen easily from the ground, were carved by a pupil. Some, in dimly lit positions, are not his work either. But the rest are his—carved by one man over a period of about ten years. This points to great singleness of mind as well as dedication to his art. He must have gone to work, day by day, as the great church rose from the apse in the east end to the final erection of the west front.

Each week he completed a capital, for it took from six to seven days to finish a historiated capital. Gislebertus carved 50 at Autun, probably from 1125 to 1126. Although a mature artist with a distinctive style of his own, he must nevertheless, when he began work on the west tympanum, have experienced excitement tempered with awe. All the experiences of his life, his education probably at a cathedral school, his wanderings during his journeyman days, his religion, work and pleasure, his knowledge of art and the sum of his acquired skills were now to go into what he hoped might be his masterpiece, which indeed it is. But what do we know of his life which led up to this creation of one of the most treasured works of sculpture in western Christendom?

It is thought that as a young man he worked at Cluny, where about 1115 he was one of the chief assistants and carved some of the decoration of the west doorway there. The splendid abbey, with its complex of buildings covered 25 acres. The church and cloisters and innumerable chapels adorned with paintings and statues, railed at by St Bernard for their costliness and ostentation, the music for which Cluny was famous, the magnificence of its liturgy, no doubt affected Gislebertus deeply. He was working, in addition, under a great master and these combined influences have impregnated the pupil's art. For Gislebertus' work shows a keen appreciation of beauty. He was able to express in stone the appeal of form and flesh, long before any other sculptor achieved this. Not until the thirteenth century did any artist excel him in conveying the sensuousness of the living form which Gislebertus achieves in his portrayal of Eve at Autun.

His work is also imbued with human emotion and it is here that he has travelled ahead of his contemporaries. The reluctance which many sensitive natures feel in awakening a sleeper is in the hesitant pose of the angel who leans over one of the slumbering kings. Mary's dreamlike, almost unbelieving happiness is communicated through the gaze she directs on her sleeping child, so miraculously saved from Herod's cruelty. There is terrifying reality in the stranglehold which a devil exerts round the neck of a sinner. All show the same humane and vivid imagination made tangible through the artist's command of technique, perfected through his travels and experience. There are indications also that Gislebertus had gathered ideas from the miracle plays he had seen during his travels, perhaps at Cluny or Autun, perhaps at Vézelay, or elsewhere during his journeyman days. The wheels under the donkey in his capital at Autun showing the Flight into Egypt are reminiscent of those on the wooden donkeys in medieval Palm Sunday processions. His cycle of scenes showing the infancy of Christ could have been inspired by the 'Office of the Star', depicting the coming of the Magi to Jerusalem and Bethlehem performed during the Feast of the Epiphany on 6 January.

Gislebertus has left no portrait of himself like the self-portrait of Adam Kraft, the fifteenth-century sculptor, in the church at Nuremberg. But the nervous tension in the figures and draperies of

67 The Flight into Egypt by Gislebertus at Autun

his figures, the humanism—unusual at this early period—implicit in the expression and pose of his figures, show us a man who was never static. Like all great artists, he moved on in search of perfection, not only on the physical plane, but on the aesthetic and spiritual also. He was a man who set no bounds to the range and depth of his imagination.

68 Wooden model of Christ on a donkey

Carpenters, as essential to the building trade as masons, often travelled long distances to work. In 1233, carpenters were sent from Reading to Painscastle, Radnorshire, 120 miles away, and were given 1s. 4d. each for the expenses of the journey. Allowing 2d. a day for six days, at a time when wheat was about 2s. 10d. a quarter, pickled herrings 20 a 1d., and ale 1d. a gallon this seems a reasonable allowance. In 1466 carpenters were still difficult to obtain, for when Philip Viart and his men were dismissed by the chapter of Rouen cathedral, it took three weeks to replace them, and even then craftsmen had to be brought from as far away as Lille, Tournai and Brussels. Philip Viart was a gifted carver in wood and had his wife and children with him in Rouen, so that it must have been a somewhat pathetic sight to see that out-of-work procession, with Viart's workmen, and possibly their wives and children, their tools and possessions on handcarts, leaving the cathedral town to seek work elsewhere.

Two fourteenth-century master carpenters were as successful as Viart was unfortunate. Hugh Herland's sons, far from tramping the roads, were educated at Winchester College and their father's

69 The Octagon at Ely, 1322

portrait can still be seen in the stained glass of a chapel window there. A justifiable honour, since Herland was the king's master carpenter and designed the oak roof of Westminster Abbey (1394–1400) one of the greatest single works of art in the whole Middle Ages. William Hurley, an earlier king's master carpenter, designed the great Octagon at Ely in 1322.

It is as difficult to learn much about the everyday lives of working carpenters as about the other rank and file members of the medieval building trade. On the road between jobs they would often put up at inns and the records are full of accounts of tavern scenes. Here the central character is usually in trouble, otherwise he would find no place in the records at all. At Windsor an inn scene is recorded on a misericord of two men, playing backgammon. Having drunk too freely they are quarreling, and one is depicted with his dagger already drawn. A similar scene is described in the records where a certain Leonard, perhaps a mason or a carpenter, is sitting at supper with two noisy Italians in an inn at Reading.

> Being unable to bear it longer when they began to quarrel in their own tongue, he sprang from the table like a mad man and attacked them. In self defence they wounded the said Leonard, and he, living for six days after, refused to eat or drink anything but cold water, which the surgeon forbade him, and so died.

In churches and cathedrals all over Europe the misericords preserve a pictorial record of the humour, the interests and the backgrounds of these gifted itinerant craftsmen. At Beverley Minster, Yorkshire, a carver with a sense of humour has depicted a girl who, while milking her cow, is convulsed at the sight of the village idiot trying to yoke his cart to the horse's nose. At Bristol a husband coming to dinner too early has a plate thrown at him by his angry wife. When, persisting, he lifts the lid of the pot on the fire, she furiously pulls him back by his beard.

Wrestling, bear-baiting, gambling; jugglers, tumblers, musicians and the game of football—all find a place on the misericords. The last is described in 1531 as both dangerous and undesirable.

> Here is nothing but beastly fury and extreme violence whereof proceedeth hurt. Consequently rancour and malice remain with them that are wounded, whereof it should be put in perpetual silence.

For the rest, biblical stories and the life of the Virgin express the devotional side of the carvers' interests. There are also subjects from travellers' tales and from the romances. But the carpenter at Chester who carved the scene from *Tristan and Iseult* must have been fuddled when he listened to the story. For on his misericord, instead of showing King Mark in hiding behind a tree—his presence betrayed to the lovers by his reflection in the lake below— the king's head is suspended from a branch like some decapitated trophy at an Assyrian feast.

Contemporary poems also reveal these craftsmen to us. As they so often had to tramp from place to place to reach their building sites, they often put up at wayside inns and doubtless, finding convivial company, stayed unduly long at some. This Christine de Pisan had described.

> *At these taverns every day*
> *You will find that they will stay,*
> *And go on drinking far too long,*
> *Until it gets to evensong.*
> *By which time they've spent, it's true,*
> *More than they'd earn a long day through.*

Yet, if ambitious and gifted, a craftsman might end, if not in the service of a king or bishop, yet perhaps as successful as Chaucer's carpenter who, with the haberdasher, weaver, dyer and tapestry maker, went on pilgrimage. They were

> *. . . all clothed in the same livery,*
> *That of a great and dignified guild.*
> *Their gear was all freshly and newly adorned,*
> *Their knives were mounted, not with brass,*
> *But entirely with silver, wrought full clean and well.*
> *As were their girdles and pouches too.*
> *Well seemed each of them a burgess fair enough*
> *To sit in a guildhall or on a dais.*

> *For chattels had they enough and rent*
> *And to this their wives would also assent*
> *Or else they would be certainly to blame*
> *For it is pleasant to be called 'Ma Dame'.*
> *And go into church first on feast eves,*
> *And have your mantle born right royally.*

Hermits and pilgrims

Langland has drawn for us two distinct types of hermits. The one, devout and unwordly, who followed the example of Antony and Egidius, the earliest hermit-monks of Egypt. These, withdrawing from the cities went

> *To live in woods with bears and lions,*
> *Some had livelihood from their kin and nothing else,*
> *All were holy hermits of high birth,*
> *Forsaking land and lordships and likings of the body.*

For these the poet has nothing but approval. The others draw

70 *Hermits in the wilds*

down some of his bitterest invective as they 'travelled on the road in troops on their way to Walsingham, their wenches following after'. Far from 'forsaking likings of the body' these 'great lubbers, work-haters and cell-breakers dressed in clerical garments to distinguish them from laymen paraded as hermits for the sake of an easy life'.

> *They hope to sit at evening by the hot coals,*
> *Straddling their legs abroad, lying at ease*
> *To rest them and roast them and turn their backs,*
> *Drink long and deep, then take themselves to bed,*
> *To rise when they please and when they think fit,*
> *Then to seek an easy meal—a round of bacon,*
> *A loaf, or half a loaf, or lump of cheese. . . .*

Both types existed side by side, outwardly indistinguishable since both wore the hermits' habit. Langland himself 'one summer season when the sun was warm, put on some shaggy, woollen clothes, as if I were a shepherd, and in this russet garb of an easy-living hermit, went roaming on a fine May morning on the Malvern Hills'. The hermit St Damasus shown on the painting of St Jerome by Cosimo Roselli in the National Gallery, London, depicts the dress of a fifteenth century eremite, a light brown, ankle-length tunic and scapular (short cloak), no girdle, a cloak and hood, and wooden clogs on his feet.

Hermits had, in fact, been enrolled into a new order in the mid-thirteenth century by Innocent IV. They adopted the rule of St Augustine and were known at first as the *Eremiti Augustini*. They increased rapidly and formed communities soon known as the Augustine or Austin Friars. Hermits who wished to live in seclusion or in very small companies were still referred to as Eremites. In contrast to a recluse, a hermit could and did leave his cell on occasions for various reasons.

Before being able to profess himself as a hermit it was necessary first for a postulant to obtain a hermitage or at least land and the means to build one. Then the consent of the bishop of the diocese was needed for permission to enter the order. Finally a religious service was held at which the prospective hermit took his vows. On 13 May 1394, John Ferrers of Norfolk went before the bishop of Norwich in the chapel of Thorpe and swore,

I, John Ferrers, not married, promise and avow to God our Lady

St Mary and all the saints, in the presence of you, reverend father in God, Richard, bishop of Norwich, the vow of chastity, after the rule of St Paul the eremite. In the name of the Father, the Son and the Holy Ghost.

John's new garments and his crook, ressembling that of a shepherd, were blessed and sprinkled with holy water, psalms were sung and prayers offered that he would worthily follow the life of a hermit. Not all so dedicated withdrew completely from the world. Indeed many hermit's cells were on busy highroads, and were often substantial buildings. Sometimes they were donated with land attached, and sometimes a pension in addition, so that perpetual prayers could be offered in the chapel for the souls of the donor and his kin. On 5 June 1356, for instance, Edward III granted to Brother Regnier, hermit of the Chapel of St Mary Magdalen without Salop, a plot of waste called Shelcrosse near the chapel, for him and his successors for their habitation, and to find a chaplain to pray in the chapel for the king's soul. An elaborately built stone hermitage is illustrated in the medieval romance, *The History of Lancelot*. The knight and his

71 Sir Lancelot and a hermit

physician are receiving the final blessing of the holy man at the door of the hermitage where they had passed the night. On the other hand a mere wattle bothy could shelter a hermit, or a cave in a cliff. Sir Robert's cell at Knaresborough, Yorkshire, is a good example of the latter. Originally a monk at Fountains Abbey, Robert had gone in about 1200 to live as a hermit at Knaresborough. The cave which became his cell is in the cliff by the river. The ceiling has been groined and the cave has a semi-octagonal apsidal recess at the east end for the altar. On the north wall in an alcove is a seat, and near-by a piscina and a credence. Opposite are several sculptured heads, an ogival niche and a cupboard, while a gravestone is let into the floor.

Some hermit cells were built near fords, or at important bridges. Dominic, the Spanish hermit-saint, built his hermitage on the pilgrim route to Compostella and it is reputed that he himself paved the way between Nájera and Redecilla where he is buried. He also begged for money to build the bridge over the Giera between Nájera and Burgos, where he erected an oratory to the Blessed Virgin. Indeed, it was recognised that hermits took a special interest in making and maintaining bridges and roads, so that we find Edward III in 1364 authorising our well-beloved William Philippe, the hermit living on the lower slope of Highgate Hill, to levy tolls for the repair of the Hollow Way from our people passing between Highgate and Smithfield.

The hermit-shepherd Bénézet, as we have already seen, also devoted much of his life towards the building of the famous bridge at Avignon, named after him, going about preaching and begging for funds for this purpose.

Hermits also founded hospices for pilgrims, for the sick, the destitute and lepers and might often have been met on the road taking one of these unfortunates for shelter and attention. St John, a disciple of St Dominic the hermit, established his chapel-cell in the wild mountains of Oca on the route to Compostella to the east of Burgos. Here pilgrims could pass the night safe from attack by the fierce brigands who lay in wait to rob and slay travellers. Soon his example was followed by the establishment of similar hospices in Castile.

Many hermits were famous travelling preachers. Perhaps the best known is Peter, also one of the leaders of the First Crusade. Robert Arbrissel, who preached in Britanny and Anjou, settled in a cell at Fontevrault, in the Loire valley. His sanctity quickly attracted thousands of penitents. Soon the roads to his retreat had bands of lepers, repentent prostitutes, cripples, the aged and ailing, hastening to the saint in hope of cures for body and soul. It was not long before ample hospital accommodation was provided in five separate buildings, and the abbey, built later, became famous as the burial place of the early Plantagenets.

But by Langland's time the majority of hermits were 'cell-breakers', trooping along the roads for carnal and worldly purposes, and by so doing they became vow-breakers in addition. Pilgrims, on the other hand, were compelled by their vows to travel in order to visit, not only the shrine of their special choice, but also the many holy places which lay on their route. For there were thousands of local shrines in Christendom, each famous and revered, each with its long lists of miracles performed there, and each issuing its own particular images and badges. To these shrines, medieval people of every class journeyed, sometimes singly, but more often in the company of other pilgrims.

The great age of pilgrimages was undoubtedly the eleventh century, although a French monk of that time has recorded that popular pilgrimages to Jerusalem began in France in the mid-tenth century. There had been Christian pilgrimages to the Holy Land since the third century, but not on any large scale. This monk, however, tells of a Hugh of Limoges, who, having built up wide estates through violence, went to Jerusalem 'almost before anyone else had done so', to try to expiate his many crimes. Fulk Nerra, Count of Anjou (987–1040) and Richard II, Duke of Normandy, his equally ferocious contemporary, trod the pilgrim's path with the same end in view. But the reasons for men and women leaving the comparative comfort or safety of their homes to undertake often arduous and dangerous journeys were as varied as the temperaments and circumstances of the pilgrims themselves. Ardent spiritual love or dire spiritual and physical need, love of travel and adventure, political and commercial motives and even starkest fear especially in times of plague, drove them to trudge the wildest roads, to cross precipitous mountains and deep gorges, to sail pirate-infested and stormy seas, to seek and—they hoped—to find.

The three major shrines on which western Christendom pinned its surest hopes were those of the Holy Sepulchre in Jerusalem, the shrines of St Peter and other martyrs in Rome, and the tomb of St James of Compostella in northern Spain. Many first-hand accounts of their travels have been left by the pilgrims themselves. One of the earliest of these journeys, that of the violent Richard II, Duke of Normandy, was led by the saintly abbot Richard of St Vanne of Verdun. Groups from Angoulême and other places joined it, so it was a large party which took the land route through Hungary, in 1026, where the fierce Asiatic Magyars were being converted into peaceful Christians under king Stephen. There they met the hermit Gerard whose missionary zeal was to bring him twenty years later to a martyr's death.

After six months of arduous travel the party reached Jerusalem and here the saintly abbot was overcome on 'beholding the venerable places towards which he had so long journeyed, longing for the sight of them, yet, his biographer adds, its is not for me to describe the flow of tears with which he watered them.' This emotion was typical of the change which was taking place in the religious attitude of Christendom during the eleventh century. Indeed without this change in sentiment, this increase in devotion shown in action by the growing stream of pilgrims, Pope Urban II would not have had such an enthusiastic response to his call for the First Crusade. The tears of the tenth and eleventh centuries were the source of the later river of devotion and action which built churches, lazar houses and hospitals and carried Crusaders to *Outremer* to set free the Holy Sepulchre from the domination of the Turks.

The penetential pilgrimage which Henry II of England made to St Thomas' tomb at Canterbury stems from a similar emotional source. The King, while fighting his rebellious sons in Normandy heard that the Scots had invaded northern England. His share in the death of St Thomas weighed heavily on his conscience. He returned to Canterbury in haste and began a fast on bread and water. At St Dunstan's church, after donning a hair shirt, and pilgrim's robe, he walked bare-foot to the cathedral, leaving behind a trail of bloody footsteps. After confessing, he knelt at the martyr's shrine to receive five strokes from the prelates and three each from the eighty monks. All night he prayed on the stone floor. Not surprisingly, on returning to London he fell ill, but was told during the night that the Scots were crushed, their king captured and his own rebel sons had ceased their attacks. In addition, a Flemish fleet bound for the invasion of England had been driven back by storms. At once Henry vowed 20 silver marks to the Harbledon alms-houses in Canterbury—a bequest still paid after 800 years.

The token of St Thomas bought by pilgrims was a metal ampulla containing the diluted blood of the saint. It bore the words, 'Thomas makes the best doctor for the worthy sick'. Each shrine had its own emblem. Jerusalem pilgrims wore a palm leaf. At Compostella they bought a leaden replica of the shell of St James, at Amiens the head of John the Baptist fashioned into a brooch.

72 *Pilgrim badge from the shrine of St Thomas at Canterbury*

Rome sold the vernicle or kerchief of St Veronica as a badge, and Rocamadour a small image of the Virgin.

An early account of the Russian Abbot Daniel describes the state of the Holy Land in 1106 and 1107, soon after its conquest by the first crusaders. The Abbot's restless conscience drove him to Jerusalem. 'Ill at ease by reason of my many sins, I was seized first with the idea, then with impatient yearning to behold the Sacred City and the Promised Land.' He went from Constantinople by Ephesus, Patmos and Cyprus to Jaffa where he and his companions disembarked and journeyed by donkeys hired from Saracens to Lydda, three miles inland.

> There are many springs at this place, Daniel tells us, near to which pilgrims rest for the night in great fear, for the town is deserted. It is near to Ascalon from whence Saracens issue and massacre pilgrims on their way. . . . The road to Jerusalem is over rocky mountains and is a frightful and troublesome one.

In the mountains near Bethlehem pilgrims, unless escorted by a Saracen chief and his retinue, would be attacked by brigands. The road from Jerusalem to Galilee was equally dangerous, while Christians journeying to Nazareth were frequently massacred by Saracens. In the wilderness of Judaea panthers lurked, and lions frequented the Jordan valley. Yet, if these were hazards, there was a certain recompense in the goodwill, not yet become bitter enmity, which still existed between Greek and Latin Christians in Palestine.

73 Jerusalem pilgrims leaving Jaffa on asses

From the thirteenth to the fifteenth century the stream of pilgrims to the Holy Land steadily increased, and Venice became the chief port from which regular sailings were made. Between 1200 and 1250, the Senate enacted a series of statutes to regulate pilgrim traffic. One of the earliest forbade the loading of ships more than two feet above a cross marked on their sides. This was the forerunner of the Plimsoll mark. Ships of 20,000 lb were to carry 20 mariners, each armed with a helmet, shield, jacket, sword and three lances. In 1255, two trumpeters were added to the crew, also a scribe—later, two became compulsory—to record details regarding passengers, fares, cargo and so on. One chest, and a barrel of wine and one of water were allocated to each pilgrim if travelling to Barbary. An extra barrel was allowed to those going further. The space allotted to each pilgrim was marked out on the cabin floor, and before sailing, a state inspector examined the ship for seaworthiness.

Pilgrim galleys left Venice twice yearly: the Easter voyage was soon after the feast of Corpus Christi, the autumn voyage started in good time to return before the winter storms began. In 1393 four state galleys were licensed to go to Beyrout. Between 1382 and 1386 the average number of pilgrims carried each year from Venice on licensed ships was 390. Sometimes the

trading fleet was allowed to carry passengers and, before regulations were tightened, a number of unlicensed ships made the
journey. Wealthy or nobly-born pilgrims usually chartered and
fitted ships for their own use from the Senate. Henry, son of John
of Gaunt, later to be King Henry IV, requested the Venetian
Senate in 1392 'to be pleased to grant him a galley, furnished
with the necessary tackle which he wishes to equip at his own
expense in order to visit the Holy Land.' The Senate whose policy
it was 'to favour the great ones of the earth' so that Venetian
traders would obtain good treatment in foreign states, fitted out
a galley at their own expense, but made sure that the English
embassy learnt the exact amount expended! In addition, they
voted three hundred ducats towards purchasing gifts for Henry.

Between 1480 and 1483 Felix Fabri, a Dominican from Ulm,
made two journeys to Palestine from Venice on licensed galleys.
In 1480, on arriving in the city, he enquired perhaps from one
of the *tholomarii*—for a suitable inn. These official Piazza guides
were licensed by magistrates; they helped pilgrims to find
lodgings, change money, make necessary purchases and to meet
ship owners who were taking galleys on the 'Jerusalem journey'.

Fabri stayed at the inn of St George, better known as 'at the
sign of the Flute', where his host and hostess were both German.
Their big black dog always barked fiercely at Italians but was
friendly to Germans who said that 'the dog is the implacable foe
of Italians. So also German men and Italians have hatred of each
other rooted in their very nature.' Already the prickly plant of
nationalism was growing fiercely in Christendom!

On Fabri's second pilgrimage he attended mass in Venice at
St Mark's. On emerging into the Piazza afterwards, he noted two
white banners had been set up, bearing a red cross. Beneath
them stood the servants of two patricians—Peter Lando and
Augustine Contarini—who regularly licensed a galley each to go
to Palestine. On seeing Fabri and his friends, all in pilgrim dress,
the servants began shouting the advantages of their master's ship.
Fabri had sailed with Contarini on his first voyage but the other
pilgrims wished to inspect both ships. They found Lando's was
a large trireme equipped for three rowers on each bench, each
with an oar on the same level. The ship was new and clean.
Moreover when the captain came on board he set out Cretan
wine and Alexandrian comfits on the poop for their refreshment.
The cabin had space for 12 berths, but after inspecting this the

pilgrims deferred their decision and rowed across to see Contarini's galley. This did not please them for 'she was only double banked and less roomy, and withal old and stinking.' So the pilgrims agreed to sail with Lando. A contract was drawn up which stipulated that the voyage should start within fourteen days and take them to Joppa and back. An adequate crew, armed against pirates, had to be provided, as well as two meals of food and drink daily including good bread and biscuits, sweet water, good wine, meat, eggs, with a glass of Malvoisie before breakfast each morning.

Special mention about protection from the galley slaves was made. These *galleotti* who in earlier periods had been free men of Venice and subject territories were now

> big men who are urged to pull harder with blows and curses. . . . I shudder to think of their tortures. I have never seen beasts of burden beaten so cruelly. They work with bare backs which can be lashed with whips and scourges. They are mostly bought slaves of the captain, and are chained if there is any risk of them escaping.

The slaves also traded in wine and shoes, tunics and shirts, which they made on board. Their chief relaxation was to gamble with cards and dice.

Having booked their passages, the pilgrims next had to buy certain necessities for the trip. William Wey, an English priest and pilgrim wrote a guide book in the fifteenth century, *Informacon for Pylgrymes*, which is exhaustive in its advice. A mattress, blankets and pillows, which could be resold on return, were essentials, but Wey also regarded a good extra supply of food and water as necessities, 'for sometimes you shall have feeble bread, wine and stinking water, so that many times you will be glad to eat of your own.' Confections, laxatives, restoratives, ginger, rice, figs, raisins, pepper, saffron, cloves, mace, a crate of live hens, as well as innumerable dishes and cooking utensils are on Wey's list. The one chest allowed to him must have been packed to bursting! Nevertheless, since pilgrims were allowed to cook in the kitchen on deck at times, it was worth while to be fitted out for this purpose.

When the *patronus* Lando had a table erected in St Mark's square, so that his mate could enrol a crew and galley slaves, the pilgrims knew they were about to sail. They had already been warned by the Senate that it was dangerous to do so, since the Turks were besieging Rhodes and the Mediterranean was infested with their war galleys. At Corfu they heard terrifying tales of Turkish atrocities to Christians and equally disturbing news of plague in Dalmatia. Undaunted they sailed on, finally reaching Joppa in safety. Their stay in the Holy Land was short and their return voyage so disastrous that Fabri wrote: 'How untrue it is that a pilgrimage by sea from Venice to the Holy Land is a pleasant excursion without danger. Oh my God, what a hard and tedious excursion was ours.' For not only had they to endure the threat of capture and torture by the Turks, contrary winds which blew them off course, so that they suffered from shortage of

74 Fifteenth-century pilgrim galley at Corfu

food and water and the discomfort of the crowded ship, but acute sickness 'turned it into a hospital full of wretched invalids'. One knight ended his days most piteously while another went mad, dying with terrible screams. As a final tragedy, a block falling from the mast-head killed outright their most able navigator.

After his second pilgrimage Fabri visited the monastery of St Catherine in Sinai and vividly describes the journey across the desert. Another pilgrim, the Castilian knight Pero Tafur made the same journey some 15 years earlier. Tafur is the pilgrim sightseer *par excellence*. He obviously enjoys donning an Arab disguise and visiting the Mosque of Omar (which would have meant death had he been discovered) quite as much as hanging his shield within the Holy Sepulchre, a distinction greatly desired by the medieval knight.

Tafur throws an interesting sidelight on the medieval system of credit vouchers. He tells us that he was

> for some days engaged in litigation with certain merchants (in Genoa) who will not honour some bills of exchange that I had. But the Doge and many of the lords of the place . . . made the merchants pay what was mine with double the costs they had put me to.

It was most unusual for merchants to refuse to honour travellers' bills and Tafur tells us that the exchange of Sylvestro Morosini in Venice accepted those presented to him at once, 'for in this matter nothing on earth will make them delay, since merchants everywhere use bills of exchange and are most eager for fair dealing.'

Tafur also visited Rome and gives exhaustive descriptions of its ancient monuments, churches and the privileges to be gained by visiting the shrines of martyrs and saints. A fourteenth-century Englishman wrote a short poem concerning these—*The Stacions of Rome*—and states

> *If men knew, great and small*
> *The pardon that is great at Rome,*
> *They would tell that, in their view*
> *There is no need for Christian men*
> *To pass to the Holy Land over sea,*
> *To Jerusalem nor to Catherine* [of Mount Sinai]

A visit to Saints Vitus and Modestus brought pardon for a third of a man's sins. Three thousand years of indulgence rewarded the dweller in Rome for a visit to the vernicle of St Veronica, while 9,000 years were granted to a visiting pilgrim.

But, from the eleventh century, the fame of the shrine of St James in northern Spain began to rival those of Rome. The twelfth-century *Guide to pilgrims to St Jacques* shows us crowds of these dedicated wayfarers gathering in France at Chartres, Vézelay, le Puy and St Gilles, for it was safer to travel in convoy through the wild mountains of Auvergne, where wolves, brigands, storms, starvation and uncertain tracks threatened the single pilgrim. Each of the four gathering centres had famous shrines of their own, so that it was with heightened enthusiasm, often verging on ecstasy, that the toilsome journey was begun. To worship before the two shrines of the Black Virgins of Chartres, to kneel at St Madeleine's altar at Vézelay, to light candles before the image of the Black Virgin, or to pray to St Michel d'Ai-guille at le Puy, or to St Gilles in the town which took his name—this was to renew vows with all the heightened fervour which came from mingling them with others imbued with the same enthusiasm.

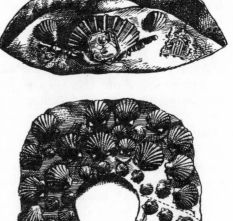

The Abbey of Cluny had built excellent pil-grim hospices from time to time along the entire route. That at Roncevaux provided beds and baths and a menu which in-cluded almonds and fruit. But most hostels supplied plainer fare, and soon the hardships and boredom of

75 *Pilgrim's hat decorated with the shells of St James of Compostella, with leaden replicas of the saint's head, shrine, cross and pilgrim staffs. The collar has shells, the insignia of the saint*

the daily march began to undermine those of weaker faith or physique. Each day, pilgrims must rise early, hear mass, have a sparse breakfast and set out with only a little bread and cheese, or perhaps bacon, in their scrip. But psalms sung en route, as they marched their usual distance of 18–20 miles a day—some-what less in mountain regions—helped to keep up the pilgrim's pace. Jokes and stories, no less bawdy than the *Canterbury Tales*, were exchanged, and at some inn or abbey a jongleur might sing the *Song of Roland*, immeasurably more thrilling when heard in the hostel at Roncevaux, where they could see relics reputedly Roland's, and where today the ancient kitchen is still preserved.

They would visit famous shrines on the way—Conques with its fabulous reliquary of Ste Foy and horrific tympanum of the punishments of the damned; Rocamadour, where Our Lady would grant them a blessing. There were many wayside crucifixes, churches and shrines at which to pray. Then, on reaching the first station of the route on the summit of the Port de Cize, they planted a cross and knelt to give thanks. This custom, started by Charlemagne resulted in a forest of a thousand crosses by the twelfth century.

Two miles from St Jacques, the pilgrims took a ritual bath in the waters of the Laventula in honour of the apostle. Also from the quarry of Triacastela they each carried a block of limestone to Castagnola. From there, carts took it to Compostella, thus contributing towards the building or repair of church and hostel there.

Enthusiasm for pilgrimages lasted throughout the Middle Ages and beyond, and there is no doubt that to many the idea of going on pilgrimage and that of fighting in a crusade, were closely allied. To a St Anselm such an analogy was abhorrent. Yet the church as a whole proclaimed that to destroy the infidel everywhere was to engage in 'holy' war, and Christians who did so were promised heaven's blessing.

12

Crusaders

On a day in April 1096 a straggling and heterogeneous army of about 20,000 men, women and children left Cologne for Jerusalem on what has been called the People's Expedition of the First Crusade. Their leader was Peter the Hermit:

> a man of short stature, swarthy, with a long lean face, horribly like the donkey he always rode and which was revered almost as much as himself. He went barefoot and his clothes were filthy. He ate neither bread nor meat but fish, and he drank wine. Despite his lowly appearance he had the power to move men. There was an air of strange authority about him.

The knights of his company were also mounted. The rest went on foot and, on good roads, achieved 20 miles a day. Behind this great, straggling company rumbled the store wagons, one of which also carried the chest of money which had been contributed towards the cost of the crusade.

76 Knight of the late eleventh century

The majority of marchers set out with high hopes. North-western Europe had not yet recovered from the attacks of barbarian and Norse during the preceding century. Dykes were unrepaired, fields were inundated or turned to swamp and marshland; there had been floods and pestilence, drought and famine during the preceding years. Could what that lay ahead be worse than conditions at home? they asked. Indeed, if there was hardship on the way, was not Jerusalem the Golden their goal and a land flowing with milk and honey? Besides, it was spring, with summer ahead. They had sufficient food, at least at first. But, on entering Hungary, all foraging and stealing was strictly forbidden. The host was well-behaved as far as Semlin, a town which faced Belgrade across the river Save. But here, a quarrel over the sale of some shoes led to high words, then blows and finally to a pitched battle. Some hotheads decided to attack the town and the rest followed.

> Innumerable as the sea, they sounded the trumpets loudly and with upraised banners rushed the city walls. They attacked the enemy with a hail of arrows so that . . . the Hungarians left the walls. The city was occupied and 4,000 inhabitants killed. Then . . . the Crusaders fell upon the abundance of grain, the flocks of sheep and herds of cattle. They seized an infinite number of horses and a plentiful supply of wine.

But the leaders feared now the vengeance of the king and hurried the vast host over the river. Some mercenaries, who tried to control them, were slain, and on reaching Belgrade, whose inhabitants had fled, they proceeded to burn and pillage the city. Small wonder that their arrival at Constantinople was awaited with dread. Yet many were destined never to arrive there. For on leaving Nish, about 100 miles north-west of Sofia, some Germans burned several mills. The rearguard of the host was attacked, and in revenge the Crusaders assaulted the town whose commander at once ordered full scale reprisals. Many Crusaders were slain, many captured, so that hundreds of men, women and children who had hoped to reach Jerusalem spent the remainder of their lives as prisoners.

Nevertheless, the remainder pressed on. Surprisingly, many Greeks gave them food, money, horses and mules, pitying their sufferings in spite of their violent behaviour. In Constantinople also the Emperor Alexius received them kindly, and allowed them to visit the wonders of the city in small companies under close guard. But in spite of this supervision, houses and palaces were burgled and lead was even prised off churches. The only recourse was to ferry the unruly host over the Bosphorus. Alexius strongly advised Peter to await the second detachment of the Crusade in their camp at Civetot. But again the hot-heads prevailed. A French company sacked neighbouring villages, seized flocks and herds and savagely slew and tortured the surrounding inhabitants, often Christians.

A German detachment, envious of French successes, later captured and occupied a well-stocked castle beyond Nicaea. Here the Turks, after capturing the only well, surrounded them. Soon, tormented by thirst, the Christians tried to suck moisture from the earth, they drank the blood of horses and asses and even each other's urine. After eight days they surrendered. Those refusing to renounce Christianity were killed, the rest were sent as slaves to Antioch, Aleppo and into central Khorassan.

At Civetot, the main body of Crusaders, on hearing this disastrous news, decided on revenge. Twenty thousand strong, they advanced towards Nicaea, the mounted knights ahead, the rest in disorderly formation behind. Near Dracon, where the road entered a wooded defile, a shower of arrows from the ambushing Turks flung the Christians into confusion. Horses were slain or ran amok and the van, when charged by the Turks, was hurled back upon the rear, which panicked and fled.

In the camp at Civetot, many children and the elderly had not yet risen. A priest had started early mass when the fugitives burst upon them. All who could fled, but with the arrival of the Turks a horrible massacre began. From the pass of Dracon to the sea, corpses lay thick on the ground. Only a bare three thousand escaped, to be rescued later by Alexius. The People's Crusade was over with little to show, except that greed and lack of discipline brought inevitable defeat.

The second detachment of the First Crusade which has been called the Princes' Expedition ended in the capture of Jerusalem in 1099 and the establishment of Latin Kingdoms in the Holy Land. Several first-hand accounts supply vivid close-ups of the Crusaders' progress. One of these, the *Gesta Francorum*, 'Deeds of the Franks', was written by an unknown, humble knight in the retinue of Bohémond, count of Salerno. This detachment marched by the old Roman road from Durazzo towards Constantinople; they stopped at Kastonia for the Christmas feast. On trying to buy provisions, they were refused. 'So we seized oxen, horses and asses and anything we could find', leaving that inhospitable region as soon as Christmas was over.

Their next action drew down the Emperor's anger. On finding a castle occupied by members of a heretical sect known as Manichaeans, the Christians regarded the act of shutting them up in the fortress and burning them alive as meritorious. Alexius' dispatch of a force to avenge his slaughtered subjects was incomprehensible to the Latins. On these and many points, such as the participation of Latin priests and even bishops in actual warfare—regarded by the Greeks as infamous—eastern and western Christians failed to agree.

In Asia Minor day-to-day conditions en route varied considerably. Sometimes the Crusaders marched through a prosperous countryside, 'full of delicious things to eat', where corn and wine could be freely bought. But at other times, as when marching towards Nicaea, Bohémond had to

> send ahead three thousand men with axes and swords so that they could hack open a route. This lay over a mountain, steep and very high, so the pathfinders erected crosses of metal and wood to mark the way.

Again, during the march across the Anatolian desert, the men suffered terrible hardships in a land which was

> deserted, waterless and uninhabitable. . . . We were tormented by hunger and thirst and found only prickly plants to eat. Our horses died and many knights had to march on foot. We used even oxen as mounts, and sheep, goats and dogs as beasts of burden.

The chance of booty was one of the major attractions of crusading, and the knight of the *Gesta* recounts with satisfaction a later attack against a large force of Turks which was hurrying to strengthen Antioch. 'We threw the barbarians into confusion and they fled, leaving many dead in that battle. Our men . . . took much booty—horses, camels, mules and asses laden with corn and wine.'

Yet of the Turks, though enemies, the author speaks with admiration. 'If only they had been Christians, you could not find stronger, braver or more skilful soldiers.' The writer played a personal role in the storming and capture of Antioch which was betrayed by Firuz, a Turk and Christian renegade. The Franks approached the city by night, then 'the men arrived at the ladder which was lashed to the wall of the city. Nearly 60

77 The storming of Antioch

mounted it and captured the towers which Firuz was guarding.'
Bohémond was slow to follow up this initial success until urged
to do so. 'Then an amazing number climbed the walls and took
other towers . . . until the ladder broke. We were filled with
despair. But we rushed a gate nearby which gave way, and so
we entered the city.' With dawn, Bohémond's banner was seen
aloft on a hill in the city. Antioch had fallen, but terrible days
of suffering followed, when the Turks besieged the Crusaders
there.

> Many of us died of hunger, for a small loaf cost a besant and the price
> of wine was beyond telling. Our men ate horses' and asses' flesh.
> So terrible was the famine that we ate the leaves of figs, vines and
> thistles. . . . This we endured to free the way to the Holy Sepulchre.

Bohémond, the author's overlord, did not proceed to Jerusalem
but stayed to secure Antioch for himself. The author however,
fulfilled his vow, probably sacrificing thereby the chance of
enfeoffment in Bohémond's principality of Antioch. Under

78 A thirteenth-century ship

Raymond of Toulouse he reached the Holy City and later probably died there.

Another simple knight, Robert of Clari, has enabled us to see the Fourth Crusade through his eyes. This was mainly a sea venture and we accompany Robert to Venice, visit the quays and marvel at the great freighters, the galleys and horse-transports riding at anchor there. As Venice itself was overcrowded, tents were pitched on the Isle of St Nicholas (the modern Lido). Then disaster threatened. The Crusaders could not pay the money they owed to the Venetians, who threatened to withdraw supplies. By promising to hand over all they owed out of the first gains from the Crusade, they were assured of the necessary transport. At this news the camp was hilarious with joy. Lighted torches were carried round on the points of lances so that it looked as if all the tents were ablaze. They moved on later to Corfu. There excitement rose at the arrival of the young, dethroned Byzantine emperor, Alexius. Soon they were sailing towards Constantinople to restore him to his throne. This dire decision had been engineered by the wily Venetians with a view to commercial profit. Instead of a welcome, the city gates were closed. After breaking the chain across the entrance, the Crusader fleet entered the harbour of the Golden Horn, when it was decided to assault the walls of Byzantium. 'They ordered their battle, their ships, transports and galleys,' Robert writes, 'and the knights entered the transports on their horses. . . . Then the trumpets sounded of silver and brass, fully a hundred pairs and drums and tabors a great many.' The attack failed and soon fire ships were loosed against the Venetian fleet. But skilful seamanship averted the danger. Another assault was planned and the Venetians constructed bridges which could be grappled on to the walls from their ships, and a way on to the battlements be thus provided.

Robert describes the attack on a postern gate into the city

where his own priestly brother Aleaumes 'was so doughty that in every attack he was the first'. It was he who led the way when the postern was broken, enabling another gate to be opened which gave the city to the Crusaders. Then writes Robert bitterly: 'The high men, the rich men betrayed the knights and the common people in the crusading host. They seized all the richest houses and had them all taken before the poor knights and common people knew of it.' The city was given over to pillage and raping for three days. Nowhere else could such a collection of ancient masterpieces, of contemporary works of art, of splendid libraries, churches and palaces be found. Many of these irreplaceable treasures were destroyed, the rest were looted. As for the unhappy inhabitants their sufferings could not have been greater had the Saracens, not fellow Christians, been their conquerors.

Robert wandered round the ravaged city, but even after its destruction its splendours filled him with wonder. In the Great Palace were 500 halls all interconnected, he tells us, all of gold mosaic. The very hinges of palaces and churches were of silver, every column of jasper, or porphyry or precious stone. As for precious relics, 'I could not tell you all the truth, there were so many', he gasps. Yet he goes on to describe the head of John the Baptist, the crystal phial holding drops of Christ's blood, nails from the True Cross and pieces from it as big as a man's leg.

But the highlight for Robert was the coronation of Baldwin, count of Flanders, as emperor of Byzantium. There he sat on his high throne while mass was sung, 'holding his sceptre in one hand and his golden orb in the other' The impressive ceremony over, Baldwin mounted a white horse and was escorted to his palace and seated on the throne of Constantinople, while all the great ones did homage. The Greeks also bowed to their western emperor, doubtless with bitterness in their hearts, at so great a betrayal. As for the Crusade, it was forgotten.

During the twelfth century two

79 Seal of the Knights Templars— two knights on one horse, symbol of poverty

80 Medal of Sir John Kendal,
Turcopolier of Rhodes in 1476

special Orders were established, primarily to aid pilgrims to the Holy Land. These were the Templars and the Hospitallers. The Order of the Knights Templars were housed within the precincts of the Temple on Mount Moriah. They wore a white mantle with a red cross. As a military order their task was to protect pilgrims on the roads of Palestine. They lived under a strict monastic rule, but the order soon became incredibly rich and, during the fourteenth century, was abolished. The Order of the Knights Hospitallers of St John first devoted itself to the care of poor and sick pilgrims. They wore black mantles with a white cross and soon developed into a military order. During the thirteenth century, when Syria was evacuated, they took up their quarters on the island of Rhodes.

The career of one of these knights, styled 'Turcopolier' or 'Expeller of Turks', shows how far it was necessary for these crusaders to travel in the performance of their various duties. This high office was held by Sir John Kendal, an Englishman, by bull of the Grand Master dated at Rhodes 14 March 1476–7. He had by virtue of his office to command the cavalry of knights in guarding the whole coastline of Rhodes. In 1480 some 80,000 Turks laid siege to Rhodes, but Kendal may have been in Ireland at the time 'procuring men and money to resist the unspeakable Turk'. In 1484 he was in Rome to tender the obedience of the Order on the Pope's accession. By 1485 he was Grand Prior of England and had been to Venice to buy oil, wine and other things for the relief of Rhodes. 'At Modon he and his ship were detained, the oil and wine plundered and his horse worth 80 ducats stolen.' The Venetian Senate ordered that in compensation, the costs of his horses which he kept in Padua should be paid to him, in addition to 200 golden ducats in ready money. In May, 1485 the Senate sent to the Venetian governors of Padua, Vicenza, Verona and Brescia warning that Kendal was about to come to Padua.

Watch for his arrival, was the order, meet him on the way well accompanied, receive him with every mark of love and respect, accompany him to his lodging where you will have his expenses paid and those of his retinue from the monies of our Signory. On his departure, accompany him with tokens of honour, making the usual offers in such pleasant form of speech as you will know how to do.

Hospitaller Kendal's duties after this date were those of one in the service of the king of England rather than of a member working specifically for his own Order. His last task before his death was to wait on Catherine of Aragon when she arrived in England in 1501 for her ill-fated marriage to Prince Arthur. Kendal therefore did not live to see the triple triumph of the Turks—their capture of Belgrade from the Hungarians, the capitulation of the Hospitallers on Rhodes, and the tragic defeat of the Hungarians on Mohacs field (1526). The Turks had now established a great and aggressive Moslem Empire which stretched into the heart of Europe. Constantinople, which had barred the entrance, had been fatally weakened in 1204. The Latin Christians of the Fourth Crusade had then sown a Turkish wind. In 1526 at the Battle of Mohacs, Europe reaped the whirlwind.

13

Parish priests, pardoners and friars

The parish clergy of the Middle Ages were far from being a homogeneous class. If one of the wealthier rectors were met on the road, riding his richly caparisoned palfrey, he might well have been mistaken for a well-to-do layman. For, instead of the sober gown of grey or black with a plain leather girdle, and over all—for travelling—a dark hooded cloak, which was prescribed for clerics, he would most likely be wearing gay, luxurious garments of a quasi-military cut. Indeed, in 1342, the Archbishop of Canterbury bitterly complained that many clerics

scorn to wear the tonsure . . . and distinguish themselves by effeminate, shoulder-length hair. They walk about in military, rather than clerical dress, with an outer habit, very short and tight-fitting, with long sleeves which do not touch the elbow. Their hair is curled and perfumed, their hoods have lappets of wonderful length. They wear long beards, rings on their fingers and girded belts studded with jewels. Their purses are enamelled gilt, their boots of red and green, peaked and cut in many ways, and their cloaks so furred that there is no distinction between them and laymen.

81 Archdeacon and clergy in secular dress

Chaucer's description of certain priests agrees with

the Archbishop as to the military
trappings worn by some, for these,
writes the poet, have

Bucklers broad and swords long,
Baudrick with basilards keen,
Such tools are hung about their neck,
With anti-Christ are such priests leagued.

But it was only the wealthier
class of priests who could afford
such costly attire. These were the
rectors of rich benefices who
might hold many such livings.
Even though only in minor orders
—that of deacon, sub-deacon, or
acolyte—they would nevertheless
be able to obtain the income from
one or more benefices. Often they
did not proceed to the priesthood
at all, but employed a qualified
chaplain or vicar to do the work of
their parishes. Meanwhile they

82 An ostiary—a clerk
in minor orders

lived elsewhere as laymen on the great tithes and other emolu-
ments of their benefices.

Will Langland, the author of *Piers Plowman*, belonged to this
second and numerous class of unbeneficed clergy, who worked
for a salary—often shamefully small—as assistants for beneficed
parish priests, usually non-resident. Langland tells us how he
augmented his small income by begging.

The tools I work with are my Paternoster and my Prayer Book and
sometimes my Offices for the Dead and my Psalter and Seven Penetential Psalms. And with these I sing for the souls of those who help
me; and I expect those who give me food when I visit them once or
twice a month, to give me a hearty welcome. So I travel round, first
to this house, then to that. That's how I do my begging—with my
stomach as my only bag and bottle.

Chaucer's Poor Parson whom we meet on the road to Canterbury belonged to the third class of parish priests, that of the
beneficed clergy who lived and worked in their parishes.

But rich he was of holy thought and work.
He was also a learned man, a clerk,
That Christ's gospel truly would preach.
His parishioners devoutly would he teach.

Wide was his parish, and houses far asunder,
But he neglected not for either rain or thunder
In sickness or in trouble to visit
The farthest in his parish, great and small,
Upon his feet, and in his hand a staff.

Even more praiseworthy was his reluctance to curse any of his parishioners who had not paid their due tithes. For this was a matter which caused constant disputes, litigation and even bloodshed. Payment of a tenth part of the produce, cattle and stock, as well as of profits, was incumbent upon all parishioners, traders and even servants being included. Theoretically, church revenues were divided into three parts, one being for the clergy, another for the poor and the third for the upkeep of the church. In practice the *rector* or ruler of the benefice, whether resident or not, retained the 'great tithes' of corn and sometimes of wool. The vicar, if the rector had appointed one to do the work of the parish, had

83 Payment of tithes

the 'small tithes', while the portion for the poor and for the upkeep of the church were ignored.

During the corn and wine harvest, therefore, heavy wagons creaked and groaned along the roads on their way to the barn or cellar of the owner of the church benefice. Sometimes this was a lay lord, sometimes a monastery, sometimes a non-resident cleric. Harvest homes were often celebrated, food and drink being provided by the rector. In vine-growing regions carts, carrying heavy casks of wine, travelled from the vineyards to lay or to monastic cellars. At one monastery food and drink was provided in abundance. Here it was declared that

> when the wine is safely unladen, then a great tub shall be filled with wine which they have brought, with a stoup therein so that each can drink for himself. But let the cellarman lock his cellar, and the cook his kitchen, so that if the peasants wax drunken and smite the cellar-man or the cook, they shall pay no fine. Then let them drink so that two of them cannot bear the third back to the wagon.

These convivial sops, flung to the labouring peasantry, no doubt helped temporarily to assuage the resentment against the many restrictions and heavy payments in one form or another which the workers had to suffer. Nevertheless tithes were always regarded as a thorn in the flesh and, in spite of the curse which the parson was obliged to deliver from his pulpit several times a year against non-payment, they were frequently evaded or paid only with the worst produce or animals. Since they were supposed to be laid upon the altar of the church, processions of reluctant contributors might sometimes be seen on quarter days bearing the required offerings. The vicar of Churchill, near Oxford—his rector being St Frideswide's Priory, some distance away—received as small tithes

> wax, money, eggs or fruit at anniversaries or in honour of the saints whose images stood in the church. There were tithes of calves, lambs, foals, piglings, rabbits, geese and eggs; of milk, flax and hemp, of apples, bees, fruit and garden produce. Also tithes of fleeces, from hunting and fishing, from merchants, artificers and hirelings.

In one case a certain vicar asked for his tithe of milk to be delivered to the church as cheese. Instead, the peasants, ignoring this request, went to deliver the milk to the priest at the altar.

Finding no one there they poured it out on the floor 'to the manifest defilement of the church and to the undoubted fury of the priest'.

In some places tithes were not delivered by the peasants but collected from them. In 1195 the bells of the village church of Paono (Gambara) were rung when tithes were due. Then the haywards marched round from house to house, gathering the small portions of honey, produce from the little gardens, eggs from another, even the grass growing by the wayside. When all was taken, the fourth part due to the church was stored in the nave and the local lord and neighbouring abbot divided the remaining three-quarters.

The reluctance of various mother churches to lose fees owing to the building of chapels-at-ease caused various processions to pass along the parish roads. At Pontoise in 1226 a chapel had been built for a hamlet on the other side of the river from the mother church at the Abbey of St Martin. When a villager died his body had to be taken across the river to the rectorial church, then after mortuaries and oblations had been paid, transported back to the chapel for mass and interment.

The mother churches insisted also on the attendance of chapel congregations on some saints' days or at major festivals of the church. This custom led at times to disturbances. In 1478 the cathedral close at Chichester was the scene of a skirmish between members of rival chapelries over the question of precedence. The contestants used the painted wands they carried as weapons and many heads were broken. The bishop then ordered that, in future, crosses and banners were to be carried instead of staves and that a strict order of precedence should be drawn up to regulate the entry of the various processions through the west door of the cathedral.

The priest of some churches also led his congregation in procession along the roads on festival days. At Easter, white-robed candidates for baptism and the chanting choir followed him. At Rogationtide, which fell sometimes in April sometimes in May, the village women and children, carrying bouquets of spring flowers, and the men banners, walked in procession— often for long distances, as in scattered parishes, churches were centrally placed so as to be equidistant from most houses.

One of the most solemn offices performed by the priest and his clerk, sometime necessitating a long journey over wild mountain or forest tracks, was that of taking the last sacrament to the dying. John Myr, a canon of Lilleshall, Shropshire, has left a series of instructions for parish priests in verse. He bids them

When thou shalt to sick go
A clean surplice cast thou on.
Take thy stole with thee right,
And pull thy hood over thy sight.
Bear thy Host upon thy breast
In a box that is honest.
Make thy clerk before thee go
To bear light and bell ring.

This clerk who was bidden 'to serve the priest in a comely habit' had been known from early times.

84 Holy water vat and sprinkler

He usually preceded any procession of ecclesiastics with a lighted taper, holy water stoup and sprinkler. He could be seen hurrying to perform his duties in the parish—to ring the bell for services, to prepare the altar, and to lead responses. On Sundays or great festivals he was on the road carrying his vessel of holy water to each house to asperse or sprinkle the people. In the manor house he visited the kitchen and aspersed the servants from scullion to cook. In the hall, where the lord and lady sat at meat, he is seen in illuminations performing his office. It was his duty also to

85 Parish clerk aspersing a lord and lady

86 A pardoner on the road

asperse the dead and in one pathetic illustration we see the mother turning back the sheet for the aspersal of her dead child. Sometimes the clerk took a censer containing incense, instead of an aspersorium filled with holy water, to perform his rites. But the errands the parish clerk naturally enjoyed most were those at Christmas, Easter and Harvest, for then he joyfully went his long rounds collecting donations of Christmas fare, of eggs or sheaves according to the season.

Parish clerks were often sufficiently well educated to act as village schoolmasters, to make a charter, or draw up a quittance of land. Chaucer's clerk is gay and worldly, with shining curled and golden hair. He could let blood, clip and shave.

> *This Absolon that jolly was and gay,*
> *Goeth with a censer on the holy day,*
> *Censing the wives of the parish fast,*
> *And many a lovely look he on them cast.*

Equally worldly was another class of ecclesiastics who went from inn to inn and from fair to fair selling indulgences, or pardons from which they took their name of pardoners. Langland assures us that most parish priests welcomed them and were in fact in league with them. For the money which the pardoner gained from the credulous villagers he shared with the parson. Langland's picture of a pardoner at work cannot be bettered.

> There was a Pardoner, preaching like a priest. He displayed a document, plastered with Bishop's seals, assuring the folk that through it the vows they had broken and fasts not kept would be forgiven. How delighted his listeners were! They crowded round and knelt to kiss the pardon. Then he, thrusting letters of indulgence at them raked in their rings and jewelry.

At fairs the pardoners did a roaring trade so that these gatherings were often referred to as 'pardons'.

These documents—known also as letters of indulgence—were during the twelfth century first granted by the pope to monasteries as a means of augmenting their income. The pardons were then regranted to those who visited the relics at the abbey church, and gave a donation. In 1252 Alexander IV gave 100 days' plenary indulgence for a visit to the relics of the abbatial church of St Colombe at Sens, and 100 more when contributions were made to the building fund there.

In 1321 the conventional church of Athelney was ruinous. The monks, however, gained the bishop's permission to send their most able preachers round to neighbouring churches where, after Gospel, they begged for funds. So numbers of these monks, turned pardoner, 'trudged the Somerset roads from church to church bearing indulgences for those almsgivers who—if penitent— would be granted a remission of punishment on sins committed

87 c. 1300 Pope Boniface presiding over the Papal College

during the 30 days, following their payment.' Friars of the Franciscan and Dominican orders became, especially after the thirteenth century, the busiest pardon-mongers in Europe. So much so, that at the sight of a friar approaching on the road, folk would rush the other way or hide. The sale of indulgences had opened the way for fraud, and there were many false pardoners who carried not only forged indulgences but a stock of pseudo relics as well, which the faithful were invited to kiss on payment of a fee. Chaucer's pardoner at the Tabard Inn calls out an invitation.

> *I rede that our host shall begin*
> *For he is most enveloped in sin.*
> *Come forth, sir host, and offer first anon,*
> *And thou shalt kiss the relics every one,*
> *Yea, for a groat; unbuckle then thy purse.*

There were many of these knaves abroad. One, a Dominican friar was driven out of the city of Exeter in 1380 by the bishop who accused him of 'extorting pecuniary gain from our simple folk, by feigned falsehoods and subtle devices under cloak of papal power committed to him. He holds up the Sacrament of Penitence everywhere for sale . . . to the grievous peril of their souls and his own.' Undismayed the friar pursued his travels into Cornwall where he continued to exercise his evil trade.

Chaucer's pardoner boasted of his prowess in preaching. Looking round at the assembled pilgrims he declared

> *Lordings, in churches when I preach*
> *I aim to have an hauteyn speech*
> *And ring it out as loud as doth a bell*
> *For I can all by rote which that I tell.*
> *My theme is always one and ever was—*
> *The root of evils all, is in cupidity.*

> *I stand like a clerk in my pulpit*
> *And when the ignorant crowd is down i-set*
> *I preach so as you have heard before*
> *And tell them a hundred japes more*
> *Than troubles me to stretch out my neck.*

> *My hands and tongue go so yerne*
> *That it is joy to see my business.*

Bocaccio's pardoner, Fra Cipolla, is an engaging fellow, with his twinkling eyes and red hair—'the jolliest rascal in the world'. He too had a feather—one fallen from the very wing of Gabriel, in the Blessed Virgin's chamber at the Annunciation, and treasured by the faithful ever since.

But devout churchmen deplored this display of false relics and the sale of indulgences. Thomas Gascoigne, the fifteenth-century chancellor of Oxford wrote

> Nowadays, sinners boast they can easily get for 4d. or 6d. a plenary remission of their guilt and penalty for sin through an indulgence granted by the pope. For these pardon-mongers travel about selling one of these letters, sometimes for 2d., sometimes for a draught of wine, and sometimes for carnal love.

Yet, at last, on 17 July 1562 at the ecumenical Council of Trent, the very name and profession of pardoner was abolished. Attempts to reform the brotherhood had repeatedly failed, so that it was decreed that 'a condition so scandalous should no longer persist among the faithful'.

But, although many pardoners were friars, yet all friars were not as fraudulent and grasping as most pardoners. St Francis and his early followers, on the contrary, lived lives of extremest poverty. Being forbidden to own property even communally, and to have only a gown, girdle and under-garment for themselves, they were forced to beg. These earliest friars had no settled home, so were constantly on the road. For, not only was it true that they 'had no precinct wall but the ocean', in fact, the sea itself did not confine them. St Francis himself went to Syria to convert the Moslems and many of his followers imitated his example. Friar John of Pian di Carpini was another traveller. By order of the Pope he went to Tartary. In 1247 we meet him face to face in the pages of the biography of the young Franciscan Salimbene. John but newly returned from Karakorum, capital city of the great Ghenghis Khan in Outer Mongolia, and Salimbene were both guests within the walls of the 'first convent beyond Lyons'. Salimbene found Brother John was

> friendly, spiritual and learned, a great speaker and skilled in many things. He showed us a wooden goblet which he bore as a gift to the Pope. In the bottom was the likeness of a fair queen . . . not wrought by art or any painter's skill, but by the influence of the stars; even if cut into a hundred pieces it would yet bear the imprint of that image.

Salimbene himself travelled constantly on the roads of France and Italy. Through his autobiography we can journey with him and learn at first hand the sort of life lived by a friar who laid no claim to be a saint. Though morally and intellectually above the average of his brethren, and though conventionally pious, he enjoyed to the full the opportunities of travel, and while avoiding the more flagrant sins, thoroughly enjoyed good food and wine when they came his way. His travels also enabled him to indulge his passion for music and all his closest friends seem to have been musicians and singers. St Francis and his followers claimed to be 'God's troubadours' and sang often as they marched barefoot along the roads. One of Salimbene's friends, Brother Vita of Lucca, followed his founder's example. He was 'the best singer in the world of harmony and plainsong'. His voice was thin and subtle, and he sang often before bishops, archbishops and the Pope himself. Once when he marched singing along a country road, a nightingale in a thicket ceased its trills on hearing Brother Vita's song. When he stopped, it resumed its strain. When he sang it listened most attentively. So bird and friar sang, warbling in turn their delightful melodies.

On another occasion Brother Vita sang so enchantingly that 'a certain nun, hearing his song from a neighbouring convent threw herself from a window to follow him. But this might not be,' Salimbene puts in dryly, 'for she broke her leg in the fall.'

Friars performed other services while journeying from place to place. They were inveterate news-gatherers, and as such invaluable as spies and despatch carriers. During the war between the Pope and the deposed Emperor Frederick II in Italy, Salimbene was one of a thousand friars who carried news to and fro.

> In that same year 1247 [he writes], while my city (Parma) was besieged by the deposed Emperor, I went to Lyons . . . where the Pope spoke familiarly with me in his chamber, for since my leaving Parma he had had neither messenger nor letters.

Later Salimbene made a public announcement when 'bystanders jostled shoulder to shoulder in a great crowd, so eager were they to have tidings of Parma'.

But a more sinister task fell to the friars, more especially to the Dominicans, for St Dominic and his order had been commissioned by the Pope to expound theology and to combat heresy. Among these heretics the 'poor Men of Lyons', also known as Waldenses, taught that obedience to the clergy was not commanded by the Bible. The Albigenses who were strong in Toulouse, denied many of the accepted beliefs of the Christian religion. On one of his journeys St Dominic lodged with an Albigensian and brought him back to the true faith. Afterwards he and his followers, the Black Friars, devoted much of their energies to try to convert heretics. Their lack of success led to a so-called crusade against the Albigensians. Soon the roads of southern France witnessed the passing of papal troops who committed untold horrors and atrocities, leaving this once highly cultured and fertile region a desert. The fortified cathedral of Albi, still glowering from its hill-top, symbolised the repressive power of the orthodox church —once the champion of reform— against revolt.

88 St Dominic

Even the doctrines of St Francis, received with such enthusiasm at first, were soon opposed and his early ideals abandoned by the majority of his followers. Yet at the close of the Middle Ages, Franciscans of the calibre of their founder were still far from uncommon. One of these, St Bernadino, had himself been influenced in 1401 by St Vincent Ferrer, a Spanish Dominican. This saintly friar was followed along the roads by processions of penitents. He had also a choir of boys, several priests to hear confessions and a notary to record the many reconciliations brought about by the saint's preaching.

From 1405 until his death in 1444 St Bernadino constantly travelled the roads of Italy. Peasants in the fields would look up from their work to see a laden donkey, led by a barefooted friar pass by, while close behind followed another friar, his shabby grey gown hanging loosely on his emaciated form. Then they would hurry home at sunset to find Bernadino preparing to preach

169

89 St Bernadino preaching in Siena

in a field outside their village. A pennon blowing from a staff showed which way the breeze was blowing, and folk gathering round would sit down-wind in order to hear more easily. For none wished to miss a single one of the little friar's quips and japes. They all recognised in his stories the *Monna Pigra*—Madam Lie-abed—of their own village and the *Monna Solecita*—Madam Early-bird—who was always to the fore when bargains or good seats were to be had. They delighted, too, in anecdotes such as that about Madonna Saragia, who gobbled cherries by the handful before her servant; yet wishing to impress her husband, she ate daintily in his presence, turning meanwhile to ask super-ciliously of her servant, 'How do the peasants eat their cherries?' 'As you ate yours this morning, Madonna,' he replied, 'in great handfuls.'

His listeners also could see for themselves, that when Bernadino preached, 'You must give to the poor gladly, for a grudging spirit dries up the bones', it was no over-fed, warmly-clad friar who spoke, but a man who knew hunger and hardship like themselves. They had seen him toiling in the fields in cold and heat, nursing the plague-stricken until struck down himself, risking persecution and the death of a heretic, to proclaim his beliefs. Through such men the influence of the friars, tramping barefoot along the roads of Europe and beyond, did much to counteract the sceptism caused by the laxity of the majority. Though these fell below the standards set by St Francis, nevertheless his ideals had entered so deeply into the materialistic organization of Christendom, that his teachings can still inspire the modern world.

14

Bishops

During the Middle Ages, bishops and archbishops were not only ecclesiastical but lay magnates as well, holding some of their lands from lay overlords by the payment of certain dues and services. Many, in fact, were tenants-in-chief of the lay ruler of the land in which their estates lay. This involvement in the system of feudal tenure caused disputes which entailed litigation and the expenditure of money and time in making long and costly journeys both at home and abroad. In addition, some of these ecclesiastical princes, especially on the continent of Europe, vied with lay princes in the size of their armed retinues, in fortifying their manor houses and in building castles.

The Bishops of Lausanne and Geneva were counted as great barons and waged war almost continuously during the twelfth century, when the Bishop of Lausanne built no less than four new castles. Even in England, Thomas, Archbishop of Canterbury under Henry II, had so great a following of knights that in his hall, straw in winter and rushes in summer had to be strewn daily for 'many must sit on the floor, owing to lack of space on the benches, and this great multitude of knights, squires, yeomen and grooms are as splendidly attired as any secular lord's mesnie.' Small wonder that many a parish priest, poorly paid, badly housed and underfed looked with envy, not free from censure upon this display of worldly power, which however, did not necessarily imply any lack of saintliness in the personal life of an ecclesiastic. Indeed, Leo IX (1049–54) not only Bishop of Rome, but a devout Cluniac monk and great reforming Pope, used a display of temporal grandeur with the express object of achieving spiritual ends. He found on his accession, that the papacy was everywhere regarded as little more than a local bishopric. Therefore, he set out with his court on tour through Europe. With his

90 Pope and Emperor and their hierarchies of power

splendid retinue of archbishops, bishops and lay supporters, he travelled from city to city challenging abuses and instituting reforms in person. Men's eyes were thus compelled to regard the Holy See as a great spiritual power bent on reform. So greatly was its prestige increased in consequence, that the papal court established itself as the powerful centre of a world-wide church.

During Pope Leo's rule the roads of Christendom saw papal legates with their attendant clerics and servants riding purposefully far and wide to denounce abuse and encourage spirituality. Indeed, the results of the journeys of Pope Leo, used as foundations for the reforms of his successor, the great Hildebrand, were fateful for Europe. The challenge went forth that, as the soul is nobler than the body, so the authority of the Church is greater than that of any temporal power, be it of emperor, king or prince. Such a claim could not be ignored. The War of Investiture between Empire and Papacy followed, as though on the journeys of Leo IX, dragon's teeth had been sown which later emerged on the soil of Christendom as mail-clad men-at-arms, spearmen and archers marching to war under opposed imperial and papal banners.

To follow the journeys of Odo, Archbishop of Rouen, in the

91 Bishop ordaining clergy

thirteenth century, is to watch a far different type of spectacle. Odo, also, had a great reputation for personal saintliness. He, too, travelled in state, though usually in acute discomfort, often in agonising pain, since he suffered 'a grievous rheumatism'. Nevertheless, he undertook in 1253, the long and arduous journey to Rome, to gain from the pope the right, vainly sought by his predecessors, of visiting his suffragan dioceses, as metropolitan, every two years. Odo's aim, like that of Pope Leo, was spiritual reform, and he well knew that slackness of visitation usually resulted in slackness of morals within church and monastery.

On the journey he passed through Mantua, where the legate wished to send his seneschal ahead to pay the bishop's expenses as far as Bologna, but this, Odo graciously declined.

> For (writes Salimbene, who was also a Franciscan like the bishop), Brother Rigaud said, 'I and my household can live on half my revenue.' Yet he had 80 mounted attendants and a proper household. Wherever he dined, moreover, his butler placed two silver bowls before him—one for the bishop's food, the other for a portion of the same sort of food for the poor. Though foul of face, none was more gracious than he in mind and work.

Nevertheless, though compassionate for the unfortunate, Odo was as vigilant as he rode about, to detect breaches of discipline outside church and cloister as he was to do so within. He travelled an average fifteen miles a day, yet never seemed to relax. Even when resting on his manors, he worked. It happened that one

St Mark's day, between Meudon and Giset, he noticed men busy at the plough. 'Wherefore, he wrote in his register, we caused their horses to be brought to Meulan, since they had irreverently presumed to work on this holy day.' The owners had to find surety to submit to Odo's sentence of punishment before the horses were returned.

On several occasions, the Archbishop made penetential journeys of 55 miles from Paris to Our Lady of Chartres to pray for relief from 'his grievous rheumatism'. He walked barefoot, and the journey took him seven days. In 1259 he lay crippled on his manor of Fresnes, near Rouen, where the king, also ill at Fontainebleau, sent for him:

> whither we hastened without delay . . . and lay that night at Genainville, where a special letter from the king bade us go no further, since he was better. On the 22nd came news—the lord our king feared himself at the point of death, wherefore we set off with great difficulty, hastening as best we could by carriage and horseback. 23 April, at Fontainebleau, where we found our lord in bed in fairly good plight.

Four days later, Odo left the palace, but by 30 April was so grievously afflicted with fever and rheumatism he had to take to his bed. 'We could go no further.'

Activities of quite a different kind from Odo's involved many ecclesiastical magnates in long and difficult journeys. Bishops were often of outstanding ability and usually of superior education in a period when there were few such. Lay rulers therefore used these abilities in the service of the state. Ralph Irton, Bishop of Carlisle, in spite of having sought and secured the Pope's support in Rome for his appointment in 1278 after Edward I's refusal to accept him, was subsequently employed by the king on state business. Indeed he was more often on the roads working for Edward, than for his see. He travelled over the fells to Scotland to negotiate with the northern parliament for the marriage of Prince Edward to the 'Maid of Norway' the little queen of Scotland whose unfortunate death in the Orkneys probably postponed the union of the two kingdoms for 400 years. In 1291 Irton went to Norham to aid in the settlement between claimants to the Scottish throne. But the following year, having attended parliament in London, he had reached home

> greatly fatigued by a long journey in deep snow. He bled himself, then, after liberally refreshing his body, desired sleep. In his slumber

the vein burst. Before anything could be done he took leave of human affairs, deluged in blood and deprived of speech.

Regarding the movement and activities of bishops, canon law laid down two prohibitions. They were forbidden to leave their dioceses without the permission of their metropolitan, and in no case were they to shed blood. Since during the twelfth and as late as the thirteenth centuries, disputes were still settled by the primitive form of trial by battle, many abbeys and bishops, among them that of St Bavon at Ghent, the Dean and chapter of Southwell, and the Bishops of Salisbury and of Hereford, kept their own permanent professed champions to fight when needed. But in 1215 Innocent III had to send a bull to 'the province of York and kingdom of Scotland' prohibiting the actual participation of clerics in this form of trial.

It hath come to our ears that a certain pestilent use, which should rather be called abuse . . . has long been held within the realms of England and Scotland and is still abusively practised there, that if any bishop, abbot or cleric chance to be impleaded by any man for offences, it has been customary for layfolk to try the ordeal by battle, then the complainant is compelled, however religious his state may be, to fight personally in single combat for this cause. We therefore, strictly prohibit such attempt . . . and any man doing so will incur the wrath of Almighty God and of His saints . . .

At a later period, John Kirkby, Bishop of Carlisle (1332–52), obviously felt justified in fighting in person against the Scots. Bellicose, yet an extremely able administrator, Kirkby lived during that period of bitter warfare between England and Scotland. As one of the king's tenants-in-chief he was bound to provide a certain number of armed knights and men, or engage laymen to fight in their stead, when the king needed them. But Kirkby chose to lead his contingent in person and for over ten years of his episcopate must have spent a considerable portion of his time in the saddle on campaign against the Scots. In September 1337, he might have been seen, riding fully armed across the bracken clad fells leading his own company of retainers and archers towards Scotland. With him went Lords Clifford and Dacre—all of them intent on retaliating against the Scots by a raid into Teviotsdale and Nithsdale. The northerners soon paid a return visit, bearing down with fire and sword against the

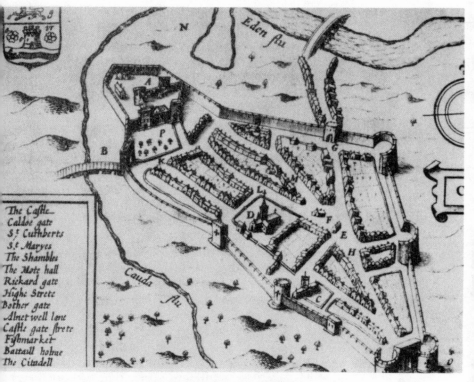

The Castle
Caldoe gate
S.t Cuthberts
S.t Maryes
The Shambles
The Mote hall
Rickard gate
Highe Strete
Bother gate
Alnet well lane
Castle gate strete
Fishmarket
Battaill holme
The Citadell

92 Fourteenth-century Carlisle

recently crenellated stronghold of Rose Castle, 'because my lord bishop of Carlisle held the manor and him they held in utmost hatred, since he had marched against them in war. Therefore they destroyed the place.'

From 1337–46 the bishop continued to enrage the Scots by fighting in seven further raids or campaigns, besides acting as constable of Carlisle Castle, an activity brought to a sudden end by the violent quarrels between the citizens and his men, as pugnacious evidently as their leader. But in 1346 the Scots wreaked fearful havoc on Lanercost Priory in Kirkby's diocese, which must have aroused the bishop's fury.

> King David and the devil being their leaders . . . they entered arrogantly into the sanctuary, threw out the sacred vessels of the temple, plundered the treasury, broke up the holy relics, stole the jewels and destroyed as much as they could.

After working similar destruction at Hexham Abbey, the English army, which the bishop and his contingent had eagerly joined, defeated the northerners at Neville's Cross near Durham, and captured King David, a source of undoubted satisfaction and rejoicing to the English. Two years later Kirkby conducted Princess Joan to marry her affianced husband Alfonso of Castile, a more legitimate activity for a bishop than warfare. Perhaps Kirkby, like Odo, the Conqueror's warlike half-brother, also a bishop, had gone into battle armed with a mace instead of a sword or lance, so that his enemies could be slain without the shedding of blood!

Yet, as Kirkby had ridden round his Border diocese, viewing ruined monasteries, churches and towns, burnt-out farmsteads and neglected fields, recalling also the sufferings of his flock, carried off or slain, their cattle stolen, their corn burned so that all—even Kirkby himself—were reduced to want, a fact demonstrated by the reduction of taxes to certain northern districts—how then could a man so much of his period and of such a temperament stand aside from this struggle?

Perhaps the same question might be asked, though with less justification, with regard to Kirkby's love of hunting for in 1340 he went so far as to poach a royal doe from Sherwood Forest, but was pardoned. The king was well enough aware that hunting with the upper classes was an addiction rather than a sport. Few ecclesiastics who could afford to do so would travel, even on church business, without their hawks and hounds and servants of the chase. Thomas Becket went to France when archbishop, equipped like a lay prince with hawks, hounds and hunting servitors. Nor could many bishops be exonerated either from the charge of licentiousness, as a very human story in the Lanercost Chronicle about the Bishop of St Andrews in the later thirteenth century relates. During a visitation the Bishop reproved

a certain vicar, of a verity lewd and notorious, and suspended the wretch. On the vicar telling the woman in his house that she had caused his disgrace, she replied, 'Wait! I will deal with the bishop.'

Next morning on meeting the prelate on his way to church she reverently bowed her head. 'Where are you going?' he asked. 'I am taking porridge, chickens and eggs to the bishop's leman. She was lately brought to bed. I go to comfort her.' The bishop said nothing, but arriving at church bade the vicar prepare for mass. 'I am suspended,' he answered. The bishop gave him absolution, and after the sacrament hastened away. Is it not too common, asks the chronicler, that those who correct others are too often negligent of their own conduct?

We are allowed other glimpses down the centuries through the vistas of bishops' registers. We see Symon, archbishop of Bourges, at Angles where 'the abbot came a league to meet us, saluted us with a glad countenance while he provided for us and our train most generously and liberally, with excellent bread and wine, meats of all kinds and other necessities.' At Bordeaux many burgesses came to pay their respects after dinner to my Lord, with trumpets, with great solemnity and reverence and received wine and comfits as their refreshment.

Another account of a fifteenth-century visitation has been left by Bishop Gray of Lincoln who was lodging at his neighbouring manor of Nettleham and set out on an April morning in 1432 to ride to his cathedral church.

> As he came near, when he was on the road about half a mile from his said city, the melodious sound of bells of the church rang out. When the reverend father approached the western doors, the bells still ringing loudly, he dismounted from his horse and knelt upon a fald-stool, covered with cloth of gold, set before the doors.

Nine canons then came out, clad in silken choir copes, bearing a cross, tapers and thuribles. The dean presented a water sprinkler to the kneeling bishop who first aspersed himself and then the dean. After kissing the cross, the dean held it for the Bishop's salutation. Then, with the dean on his right and the precentor on his left, the bishop led the canons—all chanting as they went, into the church. Mass was said, and afterwards Bishop Gray went into his palace to change from his riding apparel into garments of a longer cut.

Later, preliminary business was worked through in the chapter house, after which the inquisition proper began. Singly and in strict privacy

93 A thurible or censer

members of the house gave their evidence. They were expected to reveal any breaches of the rule, but the bishop could also cross examine them. Those found guilty of transgression were treated fairly leniently. But when the state of a community necessitated severe penalties these were imposed, as was the case with Huntingdon Priory in 1421–2. Bishop Gray had there found 'no good thing which might be likened to religion. . . . Alas for sorrow! religion is no more, love is driven out. The regular observances given to canons by Saint Augustine are forgotten.'

No doubt good Bishop Gray, like Odo of Rouen two centuries before, constantly rode away after his visitations 'somewhat impatient and depressed'. But, like him, refused to give in to despair, so that both, to the end of their lives, were found on the roads, journeying to lessen the gap between Christian ideals and Christian practice.

15

Monks and abbots

'The monastery itself,' St Benedict wrote in his early Rule for monks, 'ought to be built so as to contain all necessities within it . . . so that monks shall have no need to wander abroad, as this is not expedient for their souls.'

To many of the earlier monks, to keep this rule of *stabilitas loci*, stability of place, was no hardship. Indeed, even as late as the fourteenth century William Langland wrote:

> For surely, if Heaven is anywhere on earth and there is ease for any soul, it is in the cloister or the monastic school. I can think of many reasons for this; for no-one enters the cloister to quarrel and fight; it is a life of complete obedience, among books and reading and learning; the only person there despised is the scholar who will not learn; otherwise there is nothing but love and sweetness.

No doubt, Langland was looking back to the sunlit days of his youth, to May mornings on the Malvern Hills when he was a novice in the monastery there, to the sheltered days in the cloister when he could pore over his beloved books, for, as has been truly said, 'he was the intellectual equal of anybody'. How did it come about then that he goes on to say:

> But today the Religious Orders ride upon horses, wander through the streets, arbitrate on Days of Settlement and are buyers up of land. Today, the monk rides like a lord on his palfrey from manor to manor with a pack of hounds at his heels; and if his servant fails to kneel when offering his goblet of wine, he scowls, asking where his manners are. Magnates should know better than to transfer property to the Religious Orders, for what do monks care if rain pours on their altars? If they are given parishes, they live at ease, caring nothing for the poor—such is their boasted charity, for their lands are so wide, they think of themselves only as landlords.

94 *A hunting monk*

There was truth in this. For as wealth and estates increased the general level of the monks' devotion to their earlier ideals fell. The legislation of Charlemagne was partly responsible, for the grant of freedom from tolls and taxes to the monasteries encouraged monks to become traders. Soon many monasteries had developed their own transport system, both on land and water. Monks and lay brothers travelled far afield with their caravans of wagons and packhorses, their mules and strings of stalwart porters, crossing Alps and Appenines to reach great markets and fairs, and with them went the abbot's armed retinue as guard. Convents and bishoprics had their own trading fleets. Nearly all trade on the Loire was undertaken by the great abbeys on its banks, and those in the valleys of Seine and Rhone, Rhine and Moselle were equally engaged in commerce. By the eleventh century the Abbey of St Riquier had separate quarters for the 'merchants'. Monks went with the lay brothers as 'outriders' and account keepers. Yet all this worldly business was in direct opposition to St Benedict's rule. The whole object and tenor of monastic life was undermined by this fever to make money, which perforce took them from the cloister. Concerning this Peter the Venerable wrote:

> The professed solitary now spends his life in worldly pursuits; this cell-bound cloisterer is found always where crowds are thickest— wandering as an eager merchant through marts and lanes. To rest is torment, to sit still a labour, silence is painful and the cloister, hell.

Even more demoralizing results followed. To make a sordid profit the monk descended to lies and deception. In the early thirteenth century a noble knight, who had sacrificed all his worldly wealth and position to become a monk, was commanded by his abbot to take some aged asses to market and buy young ones in their stead.

Though hating this task, the knight obeyed. When later, prospective buyers asked, 'Are these asses young and serviceable?' he replied, 'Think you our convent is so poor as to sell our young asses?'

Others asked, 'Why is the hair on their tails so thin?' 'Because we raise them by their tails when they fall under their burdens,' the knight answered. Not a single beast was sold.

95 Water transport of goods

On his return to the monastery the nobleman was beaten by the angry abbot and monks, as the lay brother who had accompanied the knight revealed his unbusinesslike honesty.

There is another side to this view of monastic activities which relates to the world outside the cloister. For the monks' unremitting toil and their business acumen turned many barren districts of Europe into fertile regions. Where groups of miserable hovels had existed, flourishing towns grew up, where tracts of moorland had remained unproductive, these now became vast sheepwalks, so that packhorse trains left the monasteries laden with valuable fleeces ready to be treated, spun and woven into Flemish and Italian cloth.

96 Pack-horses

From the monastery of St Swithin's at Winchester, for example, monks came out one saint's day and erected stalls on

St Giles' Hill. Here they sold their surplus produce, wine and cloth. Gradually other merchants came, paying tolls and dues for the privilege. Inns were built, the town increased in size, and one of the greatest of the English fairs was established.

In monasteries and friaries there were always some monks who delighted in gardening. The famous fifteenth-century Dominican pilgrim, Brother Felix Fabri, learnt something of gardening and was always interested in plants and flowers. So that, like all keen gardeners, those monks who delighted to grow things, carried with them on their travels, cuttings, seeds and young plants. In this way monks travelling from Morimund in Burgundy to the daughter house of Altencamp took with them seeds or young trees of the Reinette-Guise apple. This, established in Germany, soon spread into Thuringia, Saxony, Silesia and Poland. The Warden pear is thought to have been carried by an enthusiastic gardening monk travelling from Burgundy, to one equally eager to experiment at Warden, in Bedfordshire.

Cattle and sheep could be introduced to different districts in this way, also. One lay brother from Citeaux was sent on business to the court of Robert of Sicily in the twelfth century. After incredible hardships he reached the semi-oriental palace at Palermo. His task done, the lay brother was presented with ten buffaloes for Clairvaux.

> To the utter amazement of all men, this time-worn man, with only two youths to help him, drove these fierce beasts through so many perilous passes, so many lurking thieves and robbers, safe and sound after all that long journey—beasts never before seen on this side of the Alps. At last they reached Clairvaux and he displayed to the wonder of all, these strange cattle which now breed freely among us. Then this lay-brother returned to his spiritual exercises and cheerfully bowed his aged shoulders to the holy discipline he had learned from St Bernard.

Sometimes the death of an abbot within a monastery took monks abroad. When Abbot Hugh of the abbey of Bury St Edmunds died in 1181 the king ordered the prior and 12 of the monks to appear before him to elect a new abbot.

> On the morrow these thirteen set out for the court. Last of all was Samson, who as sub-sacristan had charge of the expenses of the journey. He bore a letter case round his neck in which were letters of the monastery as if he were the servant of them all. So, with no

attendant, and with his frock born in his arms, he went out, following far behind his comrades.

After many labours, the 13 stood at last before the king at Waltham on the second Sunday in Lent (1182).

The king then ordered the monks to choose three of their brethren whom they thought suited to the position of abbot. They chose Samson, sub-sacristan, Roger, cellerar and Hugh the prior. These names were, by the King's order, reduced to two. From these two, Samson was chosen, whereupon, after embracing the king's feet, he walked to the altar to join his brethren in the singing of the *Te Deum*. 'His head was held erect and his face showed no change. And when the king saw this he said to those that stood by, "By the eyes of God, this elect thinks he is worthy to rule the abbey." '

Samson found the abbey deeply in debt, but by his wise management he gradually restored its prosperity. One method abbots used—though not Samson—to raise money, was to carry the shrine or relics of saints around the district. Journeying from town to town and village to village the monks displayed the venerable bones, rings or other relics of the saints to the faithful, who were eager to pay for the privilege, especially the maimed or sick in body or soul, who hoped to be healed or have their sins forgiven by praying at the movable shrine. About 1450 the bones of St Loup were taken round seven French dioceses as far as Albi and Cahors. Not all who beheld the relics gave offerings. On the contrary, a certain miller stole 33 marks of silver from the reliquary and was condemned to death. In many places, the carrying

97 Seal of Abbot Samson of Bury St Edmunds

98 Relics carried by monks to raise money

abroad of shrines and relics led to rioting and disorder, and in others during those centuries when every emotion was allowed the most free and uncontrolled expression, caused hysteria verging on madness.

It was not only business which led to monks riding abroad, for they seldom went on foot, but on horseback. Chaucer's monk kept many a dainty horse in his stable and was as hard a rider as any squire.

> *Greyhounds he had as swift as birds in flight.*
> *Of riding and of hunting for the hare*
> *Was all his lust, for no cost would he spare.*

Henry, the reforming abbot of Cluny, tried to curb this passion for hunting among the monks and decreed: 'Seeing that it is unbecoming for God's soldiers to be entrapped in worldly business . . . we strictly forbid that any of our Order, of whatever rank, to keep hawks, falcons or hunting dogs.' Those monasteries which had a customary right to hunt were exempted. It was well known to the workers on monastic estates that the abbot's hounds and hawks were often better fed than themselves. On at least four of the St Gall manors in 1441, the Abbot had the right to demand a loaf and a hen for his two greyhounds and his hawk, whenever he paid them a visit.

The use of horses was essential however to monks travelling on missions of reform. Relapsed abbeys and monasteries often lay long distances from the reforming house. Martin v. Senging, who was sent to reform the monastery of Bursefeld in 1457 when writing to a fellow monk, shows the importance of reliable horses.

> I came successfully hither to Bursfeld by the King's highway, the weather, men and beasts serving me happily to that end, for my mare is in good health and strong of body. I had to stay six days at Walsec awaiting another horse, in Regensburg three, awaiting companions for greater security. In Nuremberg seven where I believe Master Conrad, who later became a monk, would have bought me a horse at his own expense without any hope of repayment.

Bursfeld was one of the monasteries of Germany which had been reformed about 1430. One of the monks who did most for this reforming movement in Germany was Johann Busch. He had joined the Austin Canons of Windesheim, but in 1437 started out on his series of missionary journeys which resulted in the reform of many monastic houses.

He travelled first through Friesland, still one of the wildest and least developed parts of Europe. He writes: 'Since there are few trees in Friesland, the winter winds blew all around us and bitter frosts reigned there.' In St Martin's monastery where he had been sent, life was hard and the water impure. Busch fell ill. On recovering, he went to reform a house at Beverwjk, then from there to a nunnery in Holland. In 1437 he went to Sülte in Hildersheim.

> The whole land was plague stricken then, especially Hildersheim. In Wittenberg I caught the sickness. On recovering I went on to Sülte where I came at eventide and was received by the provost very kindly in the kitchen. I was told: 'The priests and monks have come from the city full of strong ale. They are sitting in the galilee outside the church. If this father goes to them they will kill him.'

Busch, however, was used to every sort of opposition to any attempt at reform. The provost however, put him for safety to share a room with 'a reasonably disposed brother', where his bed was a chest, the truckle bed being too narrow to share. 'Well,' Busch thought, as he fell asleep, half expecting to be murdered in the night, 'Here is good news for a beginning.'

On another occasion, after a long struggle he reformed a nunnery at Hanover, with the help of the Duke of Brunswick. The nuns resisted by simply lying on the floor of the choir, their arms and legs stretched out in the form of a cross and bawling an anthem at the tops of their voices. They finally accepted reform, but Busch's troubles and dangers were not over. As he returned to Wittenberg he had reached a narrow defile in the forest, almost too narrow for his chariot's passage. Suddenly two armed men leapt out, shouting to his driver, 'Stop! Stop!'

> 'Good fellows, what would you?' I asked.
> 'You have shut up the nuns of Wennigsen. They will never more come forth.' one shouted, and ran to thrust me through with his javelin. The other raised his bow to shoot me, but his hands shook in dread.
> Then I saw death, and thought, 'This is where thou wilt rise on the Last Day, for here thou shalt receive thy death wound.' Nevertheless, stretching out my hand I said, 'Good fellow, we are all at one now—Bishop, Duke, the nun's friends, even the nuns themselves.'

Busch finally convinced his attackers that the nuns had agreed to the reforms, so after warnings to leave them alone, the ruffians moved off, whistling to their fellows in the woods to take no further action.

St Benedict had intended the rule of *stabilitas loci* to apply equally to abbots as to monks. He himself kept the rule strictly and only after receiving a command in a vision did he consent to talk with his sister Scholastica during the one night he ever passed outside his monastery. With the increase of wealth and estates, abbots were forced to spend more and more time in litigation, defending their rights. Abbot Odilo of Cluny (994–1049) was as familiar with Pavia as with Paris. He was constantly on the road reforming lapsed monasteries working strenuously also to establish the 'Peace of God' a movement begun in France to aid in suppressing anarchy and warfare. But always Odilo longed for the peace of Cluny. Once, just before Christmas he and his band of monks, drenched and weary reached the monastery of Chalon late at night. As they sat round the fire drying their clothes Odilo began to recite from the Aeneid, adapting the passage to their present circumstances, in order to encourage his companions.

> *O stalwart brothers who so oft have conquered*
> *Lest now you faint beneath our present woes,*
> *Yet persevere, remember what our aim is,*
> *No earthly homestead but God's heaven itself.*

St Bernard left Clairvaux with the greatest reluctance to travel at the Pope's bidding, healing some schism here or confuting some heresy there, Cistercian abbots also met periodically at Clairvaux and had to travel widely on visits of inspection of daughter houses.

In 1135 as the saint returned to Clairvaux he was halted on the road by a gathering of shepherds, cowherds and other country folk who had heard of his imminent return. Calling for his blessing they knelt before him, then, rejoicing that they had received it from such a holy man of God, they toiled back up the mountain paths and gorges to resume their duties.

Suger, Abbot of St Denis in his early years had neither St Bernard's saintliness nor humility. He lived in semi-royal state surrounded by knights and litigants. When he rode abroad he had sixty or more retainers to attend him. To see them riding by, they appeared rather as lords of castles, then as fathers of abbeys, as princes of provinces, not rulers of souls.

Many abbots who, like bishops had feudal obligations, used their retainers for actual warfare to support their own interests or those of their patrons. During the civil wars in thirteenth century Italy, San Prospero at Reggio was one of the wealthiest abbeys in the country. In 1286 the Boiardi suspected the Abbot of helping their enemies and Salimbene recounts:

> that the Abbot was a good man with regard to God's affairs, but miserly in the matter of food for his monks. Those whom he had treated badly plotted with Boniface Boiardi to help him to take the monastery by assault.
>
> Forty good men of Reggio, however, promised to aid the Abbot, but when the dinner hour came, he neither thanked them nor invited them to dine, but sent them to their houses. Then lo, as he sat at meat, the traitor monks rang the campanile bell. His secular enemies at once stormed the abbey. The Abbot flung himself from a window, waded through the city moat and came, trembling as a rush in water, to the Franciscan friary. Later, he rode to his brother's, where he was reproached for his avarice which had brought all his misfortunes upon him.

Abbot Samson preferred guile to force in dealing with his problems. In 1198 he set out from Bury St Edmunds for the exchequer court to frustrate, if possible, the dismantlement of St Edmund's shrine which had been demanded as a contribution

99 Satire of a monk in the stocks with his mistress

towards the ransom of Richard I. When his turn came to speak in court,

> the Abbot rose and said, 'Know for truth, this shall never be done by me . . . but I will open the doors of the church, let him enter who will, let him approach who dares! And all the justices answered with oaths, 'I will not come near it.' And when this had been said, the shrine was not stripped, nor was a ransom paid for it.

In the same year Samson faced a more difficult task, one which took him overseas. Richard ordered all his abbots and bishops to send men to aid him against the French king. The Abbot summoned four of his knights and told them to join the king in Normandy with horses and arms. They, however, declared they were not liable for foreign service.

> The Abbot decided to cross the sea at once. There, wearied with many labours and expenses, and with the many gifts he gave to the King, was yet unable to satisfy him. The King required men, not money.
> The Abbot then offered four mercenary knights, but friends ad-

vised him to come to terms that he should be quit of them after 40 days. So the abbot gave 100 for quittance to the king, and returned to England in high favour with his lord.

In the days when monastic rules were strictly kept, a story is told by Caesarius of Heisterbach of Abbot Ulrich of Steinfeld, which illustrates his interpretation of the rule of chastity.

The Abbot, riding abroad one day with one of the youths reared in the monastery, chanced to meet a fair maiden. To test the young novice the Abbot drew rein and courteously saluted her. Later, the abbot asked, 'Was not that a comely maiden?'

'Most comely,' was the reply.

'But sad she had but one eye,' the Abbot said.

'In truth lord, she had two eyes, for I looked somewhat closely into her face.'

'And I,' the indignant Abbot answered, 'will look somewhat closely into thy bare back. Thou shouldst not even have known whether she was male or female.'

Such strictness was unusual. Indeed many worldly abbots, far from enforcing the rule of chastity in others, themselves were living profligate lives on abbey manors and riding abroad in pursuit of their own dissolute pleasures. Such a one was Roger Norreis, 'proud, arrogant in word, treacherous in act . . . a scorner of the monastic rule . . . a friend of women and lover of horses.'

In 1191, he was appointed by royal influence as Abbot of Evesham in England—an abbey of the first rank which had been reformed by the previous abbot and was prosperous and efficient. Roger proceeded to appropriate the monastic revenues and dissipate its treasures, using the wealth gained to live on the monastery manors for months at a time. There his life was 'violent and lecherous beyond all monks in England'. At last, the Bishop of Worcester insisted on reform, Roger consequently had to defend himself at Worcester, Lincoln, London and finally at Rome. The monks, anxious to prevent their abbey being put under episcopal domination appointed Thomas de Marleberge, one of the brethren formerly trained to the law, to defend them. Both monk and abbot had travelled thousands of miles before this litigation ended. But while Thomas reached Rome in 40 days, Roger took five months. He was imprisoned in Châlons on a charge that would have brought dishonour on his order if revealed! Thomas finally won his case. Evesham retained its independence but, on the victorious Roger's return, the sufferings of the monks continued. So bad did conditions become that 30 monks left the monastery in protest, marching from the abbey, all on foot, with loins girded and staves in their hands. The Abbot followed with armed and mounted supporters, overtaking the rebels on Wickwane Hill. 'They drew their swords and attacked certain brethren who smote them manfully with their staves. Those armed were driven back. So we again marched forward, giving thanks to God.'

Further along the road, the Abbot, 'from his own lands gave us fair words again'. The monks were finally persuaded to return. At last the papal legate made a visitation of the Abbey. Thomas was called upon to give evidence of the abbot's corruption and depravity which resulted in Roger's deposition and the appointment after an interval of Thomas in his stead. It should not be forgotten, however, that an abbot as evil as Roger was often appointed by secular rulers or, if by ecclesiastical magnates, for political reasons. The resulting waste of the abbey's material resources, and more serious, of the destruction of spiritual life was not therefore surprising.

With Abbot Roger and his successor, Thomas de Marleberge, the long procession of travellers, moving across a medieval landscape, ends. Their journeys and activities have revealed aspects, many of them unusual, of an age fundamentally different in its characteristics from that which preceded it, and even more fundamentally different from that which has followed.

The dominating influence on the lives and outlook of all these medieval travellers, whether devout or impious, was the faith of the Roman Catholic Church, since its tenets permeated medieval society. When this was undermined the modern age had begun; so that we must agree with the late Dr Barry, an orthodox Catholic historian when he writes: 'In truth, it was not the Revival of Learning which shook Europe to its base, but the assault on a complicated and decaying system in which politics, finance and privileges were blended with religion.' It was the Abbot Rogers and their like, together with the policies of those who appointed them, which brought about the Reformation, which in turn ushered in the New Age.

Chronology

Rulers and Popes	Religious and Monastic	Military and Political
936–973 Otto I		
	945–1003 Gerbert	
		955 Otto I's victory at Lechfeld
		975 Fraxinetum, Moor's strong hold destroyed
983 Otto II died **983–1002** Otto III		
999–1003 Gerbert as Pope Sylvester II	**994–1049** Odilo of Cluny	
		1020–63 Norman Conquest of S. Italy
	1028 Death of Fulbert of Chartres	
		1056–1125 War of Investiture **1061–91** Normans conquer Sicily from Arabs
1066 Harold, King of Norway slain at Stamford Bridge		
	1070–87 Lanfranc, Archbishop of Canterbury **1079–1142** Abelard	**1071** Battle of Manzikert. Byzantium lost Asia Minor to Turks
1073–85 Pope Gregory VII (Hildebrand) **1080–1100** (anti-pope) Clement 'III' **1088–99** Urban II		
	1090–1153 Bernard of Clairvaux	**1095** First Crusade
1108–37 Louis VI of France	**1109** Death of St Anselm	
	1122–51 Suger, Abbot of St Denis	
1130 Papal Schism	**1130** Adelard of Bath returned to England **1141** Peter the Venerable in Spain *c.* **1150** Universities of Paris and Oxford founded **1153**–*post* **1204** Peter of Blois	**1147–9** Second Crusade
1154 Death of Roger the Great, King of Sicily		
	1170 Death of Godric of Finchale	
		1189–92 Third Crusade

Artistic and Literary	Scientific, Geographical and Commercial	British Rulers and Events
	921 Ahmad bin Judhlan visited Scandinavian settlement on the Volga	**924** Athelstan **939** Edmund **946** Edred
		959 Edgar, King of All England **975** Edward the Martyr **978** Murder of Edward. Accession of Ethelred
	1000 Leif of Iceland reaches Vinland	**1016** Canute, King of England
		1042 Edward the Confessor
		1066 Harold Godwinson defeated by William of Normandy at Hastings
c. **1090** Song of Roland written	**1081** Venice extorts trading right from Byzantine Empire	**1087** William II
		1100 Henry I
1114–87 Gerard of Cremona *c.* **1115–80** John of Salisbury		
		1135 Stephen
		1152 Eleanor of Aquitaine Henry later King Henry II of England 1154–89
		1170 Murder of Thomas Becket **1189** Richard I **1199** John

Rulers and Popes	Religious and Monastic	Military and Political
1209 Pope Innocent III v Albigensians **1212–50** Emperor Frederick II **1226–70** St Louis of France	**1209–29** Crusade v Albigensians **1214** Dominican Order founded **1223** Franciscan Order founded	**1204** Fourth Crusade. Sack of Constantinople **1206–27** Reign of Ghengiz· Khan **1244** Final loss of Jerusalem
		1261 Greeks retake Constantinople **1271** Battle of Manzikert
1309–76 Papcy removes to Avignon, 'Babylonish Captivity'	**1312** Knights Templars suppressed	
		1356 Battle of Poitiers **1360** Peace of Bretigny
1380–1422 Charles VI of France	**1378** Richard Rolle, hermit and mystic **1390** Henry, earl of Derby on Prussian crusade **1392** He goes to Jerusalem **1408** Richard earl of Warwick goes to Jerusalem	
1419 Philip the Good of Burgundy	**1444** Death of St Bernadino of Italy	**1453** Turks capture Constantinople **1477** Charles the Bold of Burgundy defeated at Nancy by the French

Artistic and Literary	Scientific, Geographical and Commercial	British Rulers and Events
1209 Isembert finished London Bridge		
		1215 Magna Carta **1216** Henry III
	1245 John of Pian di Carpini reaches Karakorum	
c. **1250** Villard de Honnecourt	**1254** Willian of Rubruck at Karakorum **1255–69** Nicolo & Maffei Polo in China	
1265 Dante born		
	1271–92 Marco Polo in China	
1280–90 The Story of Burnt Njal written, one of the last Icelandic sagas		**1272–1307** Edward I **1290** Death of the Maid of Norway
1304–74 Petrarch		**1305** William Wallace executed **1307** Edward II
1337–1410 Jean Froissart *c.* **1342** Geoffrey Chaucer born **1344–50** Bocaccio wrote The Decameron		**1327** Edward III **1346** Battle of Nevilles Cross **1346–1453** The Hundred Years War
c. **1370** Wm. Langland wrote Piers the Ploughman *c.* **1370–1450** John Lydgate, poet		**1377** Richard II
	1380–1405 Rule of Timur (Tamerlane)	**1381** Peasants' Revolt **1396** Cheshire rising v. John of Gaunt **1399** Henry IV
1402 Christine de Pisan		*c.* **1400** Death of Chaucer **1413** Henry V
	1415–61 Henry the Navigator of Portugal	**1422** Henry VI
	1492 Columbus discovers America **1498** Vasco da Gama finds the sea-route to India	

197

Select Bibliography

General

C. Brooke, *Europe in the Central Middle Ages,* Longmans, 1964
Cambridge Medieval History (Vols. 1–8), Cambridge, 1911–36
J. Evans (Ed.), *The Flowering of the Middle Ages,* Thames and Hudson, 1966
H. A. L. Fisher, *A History of Europe* (Vol. 1), Fontana Library, 1964
J. J. Jusserand, *English Wayfaring Life in the Middle Ages,* Fisher Unwin, 1899
W. Langland, *Piers the Ploughman,* Penguin, 1959
C. McEvedy, *Atlas of Medieval History,* Penguin, 1968
R. W. Southern, *The Making of the Middle Ages,* Hutchinson, 1965

Roads, Bridges and Hospitality

H. S. Bennett, *The Pastons and their England* (Chs. X and XI), Cambridge, 1932
W. C. Firebaugh, *Inns of the Middle Ages,* Pascal Covice, Chicago, 1924
Francisque Michel, *La Grande Bohème* (Vol. 1), Paris, 1851
M. Postan (Ed.), *Cambridge Economic History of Europe* (Vol. II), Cambridge, 1952
R. L. Storey, *The End of the House of Lancaster* (Appendix I, Robert Goodgroom's Tale), Barrie and Rockliff, 1966

Sea-routes, Ports and Ships

E. H. Byrne, *Genoese Shipping,* Cambridge, Mass., 1930
Cambridge Economic History of Medieval Europe (Vols. 2 and 3), Cambridge, 1952
F. C. Hodgson, *Venice,* Geo. Allen, 1910
B. Landström, *The Ship,* Allen and Unwin, 1968
F. C. Lane, *Andrea Barbarigo,* John Hopkins, Baltimore, 1944
M. Letts, *Bruges and its Past,* Beyaert and Berry, 1924
—— *Genoa,* Methuen, 1908
M. Letts, (tr.) *Travels of Pero Tafur,* Geo. Routledge, 1926

Merchants and Explorers

Cambridge Economic History of Europe (Vol. II), Cambridge, 1952

G.W. Dassent (tr.), *The Story of Burnt Njal,* Everyman, 1957

J. and F. Gies, *Life in a Medieval City,* (Troyes in 1250), Arthur Barker, 1969

M. Komroff (Ed.), *Contemporaries of Marco Polo,* Cape, 1928

F.C. Lane, *Andrea Barberigo,* John Hopkins, Baltimore, 1944

M. Letts (tr.), *Travels of Pero Tafur,* Routledge, 1926

B.D. Lyon, *The High Middle Ages* (for *St Godric, An Early Medieval Merchant*), University of California, Berkeley, 1964

E. Maclagen, *The Bayeux Tapestry,* King Penguin, 1943

R.H. Major (Ed.), *India in the Fifteenth Century,* (for Nicolo Conti), Hakluyt Society, 1857

A.P. Newton, *Travel in the Middle Ages,* Kegan Paul, 1926

C. Waddy (tr.), *A Scandinavian Cremation Ceremony,* Antiquity, March, 1934

Sir H. Yule, *Cathay and the Way Thither,* (for Pegolotti, Series I, Vol. 37), Hakluyt Society, 1866

Royalty, Magnates and Messengers

O. Cartellieri (tr. M.H.I. Letts), *The Court of Burgundy,* London, 1929

F.H. Cripps-Day, *The Tournament,* Quaritch, 1918

C.J. Ffoulkes, *The Armourer and his Craft,* Methuen, 1912

M.C. Hill, *The King's Messengers,* Edw. Arnold, 1961

—— *Jack Fawkes, King's Messenger,* English Historical Review LVII, 1942

Y. Renouard, *Messengers of the Avignon Popes,* Revue Historique Tome 180, 1937

G. Stretton, *The Travelling Household in the Middle Ages,* Trans. of the Royal Historical Society, 1924

L. Toulmin-Smith (Ed.), *Expeditions of Henry, earl of Derby,* Camden Society, 1894

E. Vaille, *Histoire Général des Postes,* Paris, 1947

—— *Histoire des postes françaises* (2 Vols.), Paris, 1946/7

J.F. Willard and W.A. Morris, *English Government at Work,* Cambridge, Mass., 1940

Soldiers and Free Companies

Sir J. Froissart, *Chronicles,* Everyman, 1906

W. Heywood, *Medieval Siena* (The *Ensamples* of Fra Filippo), E. Torrini, Siena, 1901

M.H. Keen, *The Laws of War in the Late Middle Ages*, Routledge and Kegan Paul, 1965

I. Origo, *The Merchant of Prato*, (see Index), Penguin, 1963

D.L. Sayers(tr.), *The Song of Roland*, Penguin, 1965

Outlaws and Vagabonds

F.J., Child, *English and Scottish Popular Ballads* (5 Vols.), U.S.A., 1882–98

J.J. Furnivall, E. Viles, *The Fraternity of Vacabondes of John Awdley*, Early English Tract Society, 1869

Sir T. Hardy and C.T. Martin (Eds.), *Lestorie des Engles*, (Translation for the story of Hereward), Rolls Series No. 91, Vol. 2, 1889

M. Keen, *Outlaws of Medieval Legend*, Routledge and Kegan Paul, 1961

J. Stevenson (Ed.), *Chronicon Anglicanum* of Ralph of Coggeshall. Translation of *The Romance of Fulk Fitzwarin*, Rolls Series No. 66, 1875

Wandering Entertainers

F.J. Child, *English and Scottish Popular Songs and Ballads*, (5 Vols.), U.S.A., 1882–98

E. Faral, *Les Jongleurs en France au Moyen Age*, Paris, 1910

G. Reese, *Music in the Middle Ages*, New York, 1940

J. Ritson, (revised by W.C. Hazlitt), *Ancient Songs and Ballads*, London, 1877

C. Sachs, *A History of Musical Instruments*, New York, 1940

D. Sayers (tr.), *The Song of Roland*, Penguin, 1965

Wandering Scholars

C.H. Haskins, *The Renaissance of the Twelfth Century*, New York, 1957

H.P. Lattin, *Letters of Gerbert*, Columbia Records, No. 39, 1961

—— *Peasant Boy*, New York, 1951

W.J. Millor and H.E. Butler, *Letters of John of Salisbury*, Nelson, 1955

H. Rashdall (Ed. F. Powicke and A. Emden), *The Universities of Europe in the Middle Ages*, (Vol. III), Oxford, 1936

H. Waddell, *The Wandering Scholars*, Penguin, 1954

Doctors and the Diseased

E.G. Browne, *Arabian Medicine*, Cambridge, 1921
F. Harrison, *Medieval Man and his Notions*, John Murray, 1947
C.H. Haskins, *Studies in Medieval Science*, Harvard, 1927
J.F.C. Hecker, *Epidemics of the Middle Ages*, Trubner, 1855
Fabian L. Hirst, *The Conquest of Plague*, Oxford, 1953
B. Inglis, *A History of Medicine*, Weidenfeld and Nicolson, 1965
I. Origo, *The Merchant of Prato*, Part Two, 8, *Plague and Pestilence*, Jonathan Cape, 1957

Sculptors, Builders and Carpenters

M.D. Anderson, *The Medieval Carver*, Cambridge, 1935
D. Grivot and G. Zarnecki, *Gislebertus, Sculptor of Autun*, Collins, 1961
J. Harvey, *The Mason's Skill*, Ch. III. *The Flowering of the Middle Ages* (Ed. J. Evans) Thames and Hudson, 1966
D. Knoop and D.P. Jones, *The Medieval Mason*, Manchester, 1966
J.B.A. Lassus and R. Willis (Eds.) *Villard de Honnecourt*, Vienna, 1935
L.F. Salzmann, *English Industries in the Middle Ages*, Oxford, 1923
C. Singer, *History of Technology*, (Vol. II), Oxford, 1956

Hermits and Pilgrims

Y. Bottineau, *Les Chemins de St Jacques*, Hachette, 1968
E.L. Cutts, *Scenes and Characters of the Middle Ages*, (Pt. II, Hermits and Recluses), Virtue and Co., 187
F.J. Furnivall (Ed.), *The Stacions of Rome*, E.E.T.S., 1867
D.J. Hall, *English Medieval Pilgrimages*, Routledge and Kegan Paul, 1968
M. Letts (Ed.), *Pero Tafur*, Geo. Routledge, 1926
M.M. Newett (Ed.), *Canon Pietro Casola's Pilgrimage* (1494), Manchester, 1907
R. Oursel, *Les Pèlerins du Moyen Age*, Fayard, 1963
H.M.V. Prescott, *Jerusalem Journey*, Eyre and Spottiswoode, 1954
A. Stewart (tr.), *The Wanderings of Br. Felix Fabri* (2 Vols.), Palestine Pilgrim Trust, 1892
W. Wey, *Itineraries*, Roxburghe Club, 1857
C.W. Wilson (Ed.), *Abbot Daniel's Pilgrimage*, Palestine Pilgrims Trust No. 5.

Crusaders

E. A. S. Dawes (tr.), *The Alexiad,* Kegan Paul, 1925

R. M. T. Hill (tr.), *Gesta Francorum,* Nelson, 1962

A. C. Krey, *The First Crusade* (Eye-witness's account), Princeton, 1921

L. B. Larking, *Knights Hospitallers,* Camden Society (Vol. LXV), 1857

E. H. McNeal (tr.), *Robert of Clari's Conquest of Constantinople,* Columbia, 1936

M. Melville, *La Vie des Templiers,* Paris, 1951

Sir S. Runciman, *A History of the Crusades* (3 Vols.), Penguin, 1965

Parish Priests, Pardoners and Friars

Fr. J. P. Conway, *Lives of the Brethren,* (account almost contemporary with St Dominic), S.P.C.K., 1896

G. G. Coulton, *Five Centuries of Religion,* Cambridge, 1921

—— *From St Francis to Dante,* (contains Chronicle of Salimbene), London, 1906

F. A. Gasquet, *Parish Life in Medieval England,* Methuen, 1906

Fr. B. Jarret, *Life of St. Dominic*

I. Origo, *The World of San Bernadino,* Cape, 1963

L. Sherley-Price, *St Francis of Assisi,* London, 1959

Bishops

C. M. L. Bouch, *Prelates and People of the Lake Counties,* Titus Wilson, 1948

G. G. Coulton, *Five Centuries of Religion,* Cambridge, 1921

——*From St Francis to Dante,* London, 1906

A. Hamilton-Thomson, *Visitation of Religious Houses in the Diocese of Lincoln,* Lincoln Record Society, 1914

J. Webb, *The Household Expenses of Richard Swinfield,* Camden Society, 1854

Abbots and Monks

J. Evans, *Monastic Life at Cluny,* Oxford, 1931

R. Graham, *An Abbot of Vézelay,* S.P.C.K., 1918

—— *St Gilbert of Sempringham,* Elliot Stock, 1901

M. Letts (tr.), *Johannes Butzbach,* English Historical Review, 1917

L. C. Lane (Ed.), *The Chronicle of Jocelin of Brakelond,* Chatto and Windus, 1925

INDEX

Numerals in **bold type** refer to illustration numbers.